CNC BANK

Cimatron Essentials, 1st Edition

CNC Bank
10/27/2020

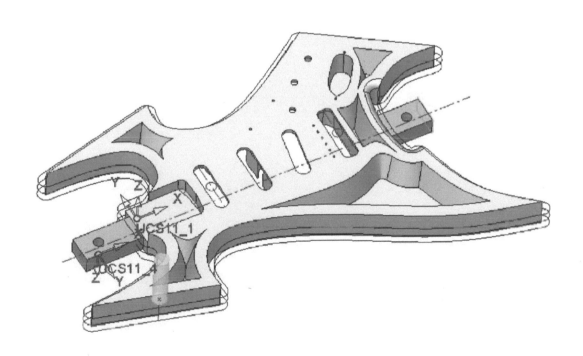

Table of Contents

Chapter 1: Intro to Cimatron

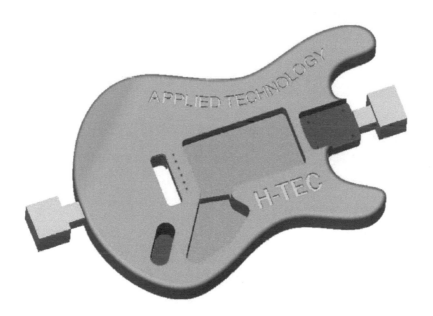

Market Overview

Cimatron is a full featured CAD/CAM application, complete with solid modeling, wireframe surfacing, 2 through 5 axis toolpaths for CNC, Drafting, and wizards for mold design, electrode design, and die design.

- The Detroit based **automotive** industries uses Catia and NX (formerly UG – or Unigraphics) at Ford, General Motors, and FCA (Fiat Chrysler Automobiles). The auto companies are *mandated* to use one of these systems.
- Tier 1, 2, and 3 suppliers, however, can use any CAD system they desire.
- The **aerospace** industry primarily uses Catia and NX.
- The **defense** industry primarily uses Pro/E (Pro Engineer or Creaform) because it was developed in the United States.
- The **medical**, **energy**, and **consumer products** industries use a variety of CAD/CAM solutions—whatever makes sense for their needs.

The Detroit area is the automotive capital of the world. Even though the auto industries use Catia and NX, **Cimatron** positioned itself as a die/mold solution to the tier 1-3 suppliers. Outside of the auto market, Cimatron is used in the aerospace, medical, energy, and consumer product industries. Cimatron is used worldwide.

Constructed from the ACIS kernel, Cimatron has the distinct advantage in the die/mold industry by offering specialized solid based wizards to design *molds* and *electrodes* in the mold industry, as well as *strips* and *unfolding* capabilities in the die industry.

Coupled with strong CNC toolpath programming capabilities (CAM), drafting, and assembly, Cimatron is ideal for the die/mold industry looking for a single solution CAD/CAM product that can design tools from parent CAD models and manufacture tools (molds and dies).

Cimtaron never intended to replace Catia and NX in the automotive sector. Instead, it decided to serve their supplier base. Cimatron was developed in Israel and is used for design and manufacture all over the world, including Europe, Russia, Spain, Brazil, and many more countries.

 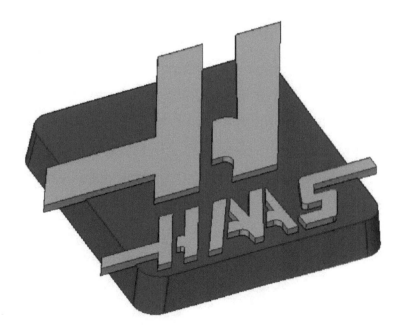

Documents

Cimatron has four file types, referred to as *documents*. Each are distinguished by a unique icon.

√ Part document: 3D model
√ Assembly document: Assembly of part documents
√ NC document: Toolpath file
√ Drawing document: Drawing file with views

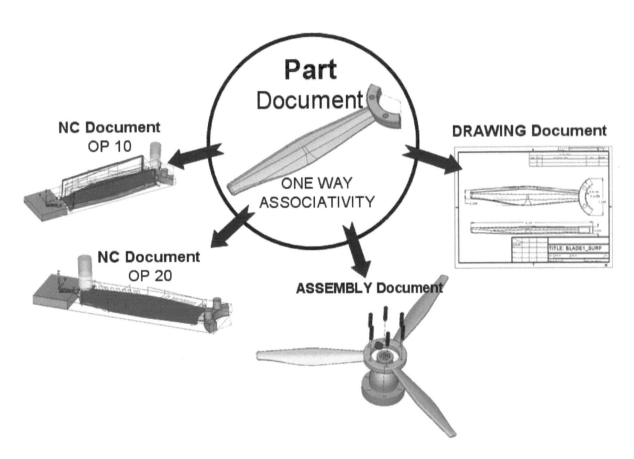

Part documents are **associative**. In other words, when changes are made to the model, they're reflected in downstream assemblies, NC, and drawings.

Kernel

A geometric modeling kernel is a 3D solid modeling software component used by CAD packages. It is the brain of the engine.

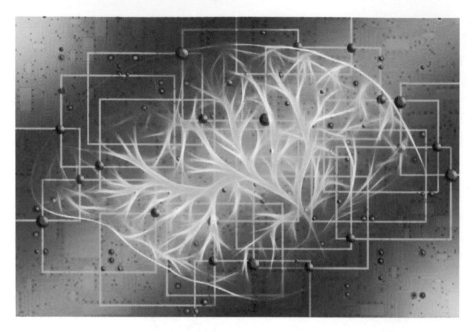

Kernels perform complex equations that produce visual representations of objects you see on the computer screen in CAD.

There are many kernels to choose from when developing a CAD system, such as ACIS, C3D, Autodesk's ShapeManager, and Parasolid. *Cimatron* uses the ACIS kernel.

ACIS is a combination of the initials of the creators of this kernel. Alan, Charles, and Ian. Therefore, ASIS is the Alan, Charles, and Ian System. It was developed in the mid to late 1980's.

Wireframe & Surfaces

Prior to Solids was "wireframe and surfaces" modeling—developed in the early 1980's when computer monitors were introduced to the market. You could develop points, lines, arcs, circles, and splines. And from these entities you could construct surfaces. The only purpose for surfaces then was to provide data for CNC machining, rapid prototyping, and FEM (Finite Element Modeling).

Although wireframe and surfaces were used to design parts, it was time consuming and error prone. When engineering changes were requested, much of the geometry had to be deleted and reconstructed. This cost time and money.

Also, designers could inadvertently construct poor geometry, with gaps and overlaps, inverted surfaces, and much more. Geometry was problematic. And because most products are designed and outsourced to manufacturing suppliers, it slowed the suppliers down as they spent most of their time repairing data.

Solid Modeling Origins

With increased market demand and tighter deadlines, there isn't time for mistakes. Part geometry must be perfect and it must be developed fast.

Solid modeling came about in the 90's to address these issues. As a result, parts are designed much faster and with more reliable geometry. Tool designers can also build tools much faster with solid based wizards than they could in the 80's, too.

Solid modeling is known for the following:
- Fast and easy modeling
- Mathematically perfect—air tight models
- Unambiguous geometry (surface normal are properly oriented)
- Engineering changes are fast to implement
- Tool design wizards (mold design, electrode design, die design, unfolding)

Solid Features

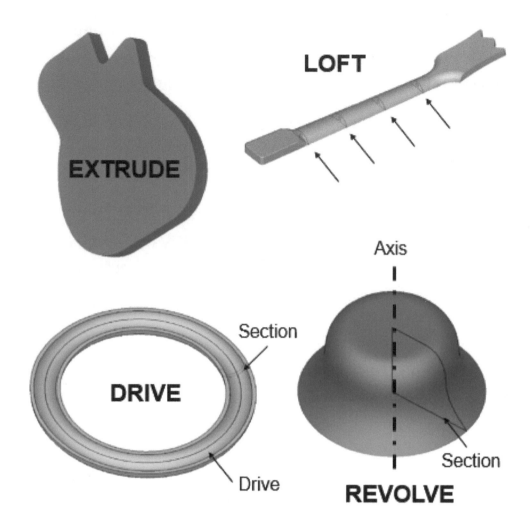

Extrude: This function *"extrudes"* a sketch or curve along a direction to a specified depth. The extrusion can also contain an angle (taper). In molds, for example, it's common to add ½ degree of draft along all walls so molds can open and close properly.

Loft: This function allows you to develop (or *loft*) a solid through each section, from section to section. The guitar neck above is a great example of when you might consider using this feature.

Drive: This function allows to you *"drive"* a defined *section* along a defined *drive* curve. The shape above is a good example of when you might consider using this function.

Revolve: This function allows you to *"revolve"* a section around an axis.

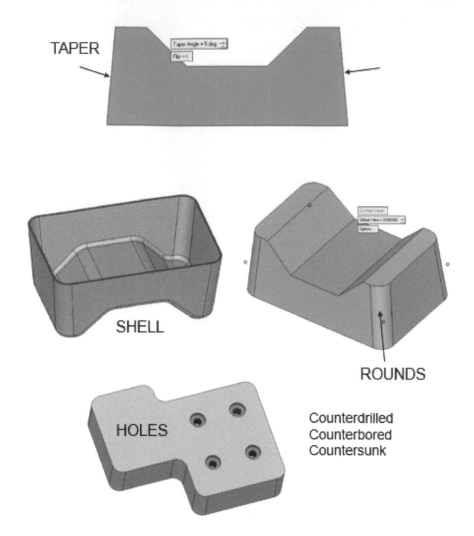

Taper: This is a term for defining angles along walls.

Shell: This is a common term used to *hollow* out an object and define wall thickness.

Rounds: This function is used to create rounds and fillets along edges of solid features. The size of the radius can be fixed or variable.

Holes: This feature allows for easy creation of holes, such as through, counterdrilled, counterbored, and countersunk.

2D CNC Toolpaths

Cimatron is a full featured CNC mill programming solution, containing everything a programmer needs from 2-axis through 5-axis.

2D Profiling (contouring) is used for contouring flat objects. The Z-axis is set and the tool simply follows along the X and Y-axis. Below are examples:

Drilling is used for drilling holes.

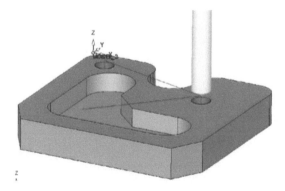

Pocketing is used to remove areas (or pockets) within a block of material:

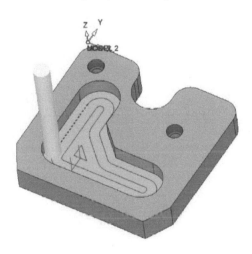

3D CNC Toolpaths

Volume Roughing is used to *rough machine* (remove) volumes of material from a workpiece. It can follow two and three dimensional curvature. It usually leaves same remaining stock for finish toolpaths that follow. For example:

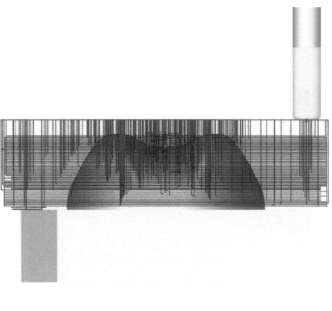

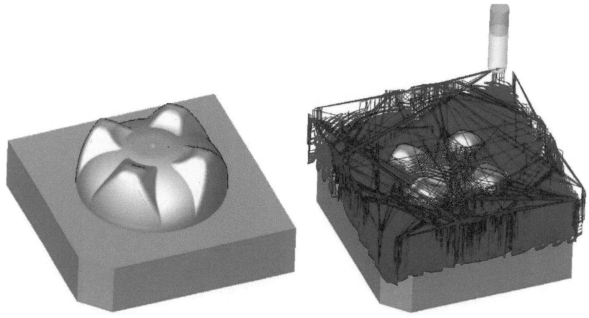

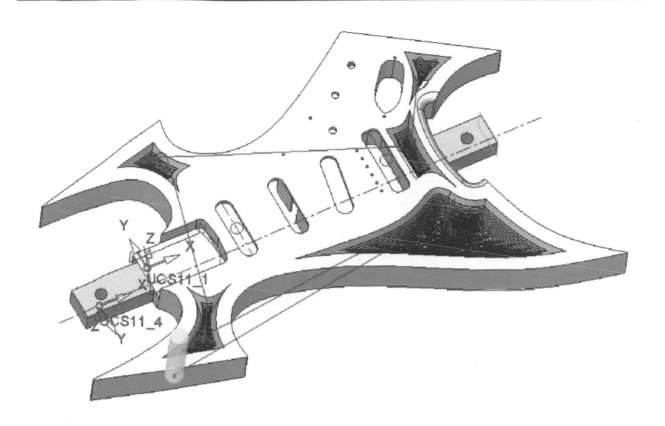

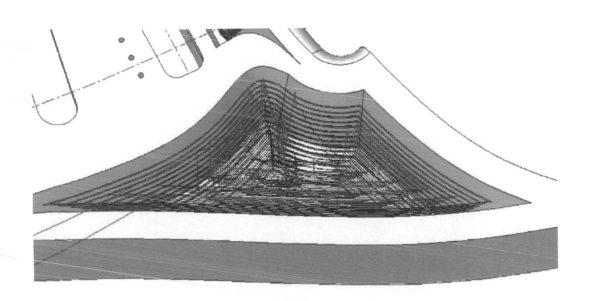

Volume Re-Roughing is used to *rough* machine (remove) leftover—or remaining material—from the previous cutting tool in the roughing operation. For example:

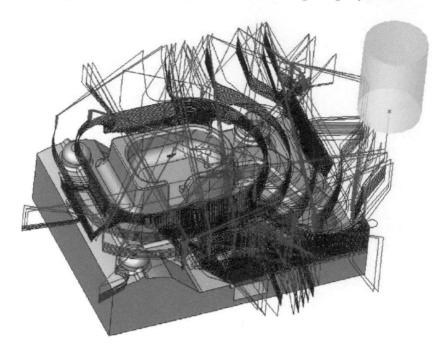

Rough machine with a 2" diameter Feed mill

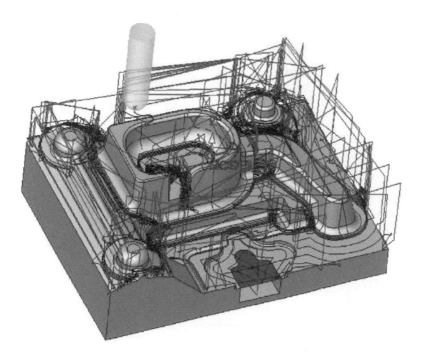

Re-rough into areas the 2" cutter wouldn't fit with a ¾" diameter Ball Nose tool

Surface Machining is used to *finish* machine three dimensional objects.

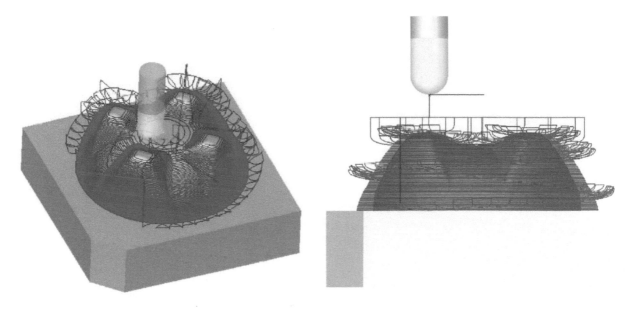

Finish By Layer (Constant Z-Level, or Waterline)

Finish Horizontal Areas (from flat to specified angle)

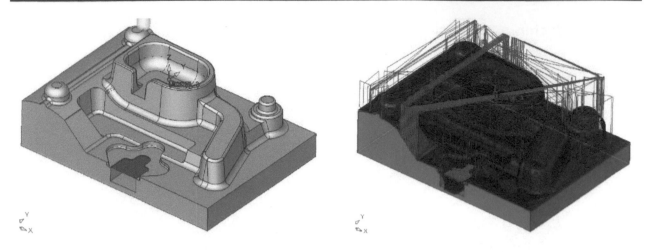

Finish By Limiting Angle

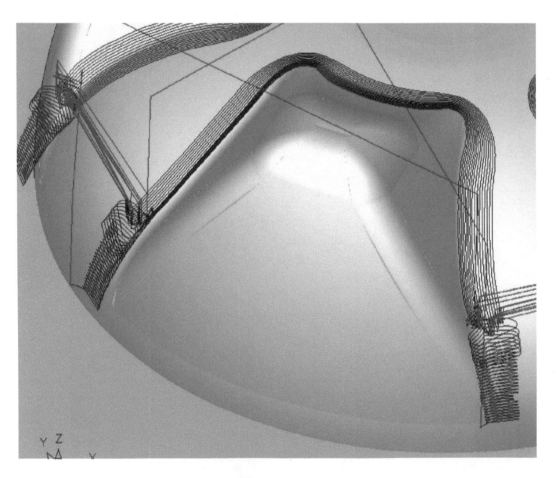

Finish Re-machining (leftover areas) with smaller tool

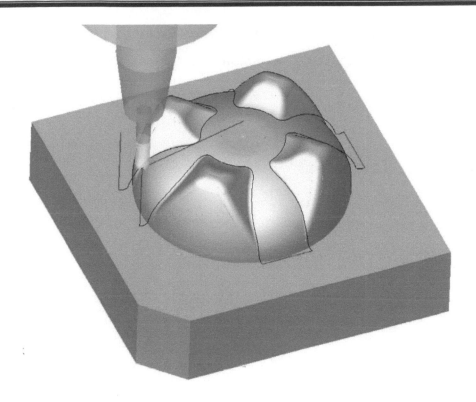

Pencil Milling along intersections of surfaces – one or more passes

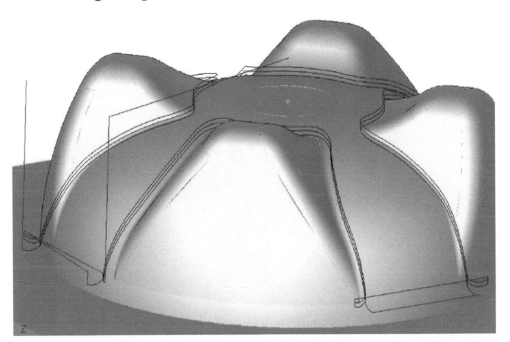

4-axis machining provides the ability to add another axis to XY and Z. It's usually in the form of a rotary table to allow machining the top and bottom sides. For example:

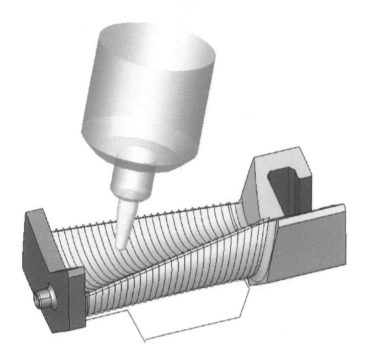

5-axis machining allows for 5 full axis of simultaneous motion. It's the most sophisticated machining. It's used for a variety of reasons, from impellers to porting.

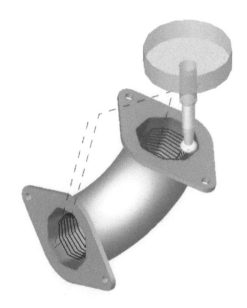

Porting

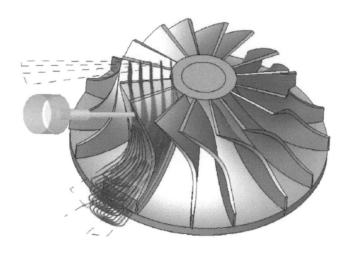

Rough machine between two vanes

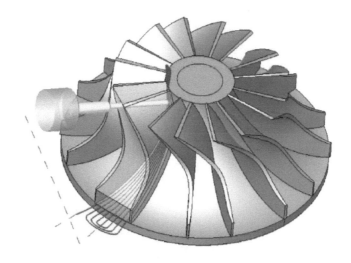

Finish machine the floor

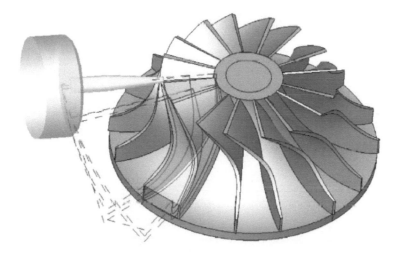

Finish machine the walls

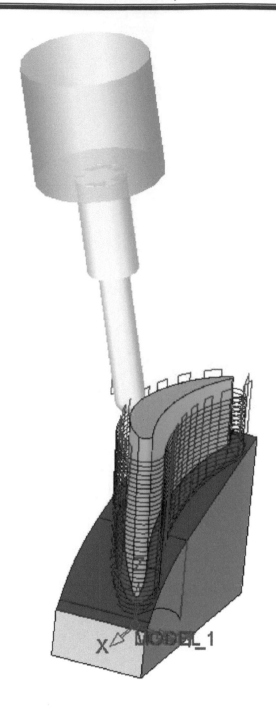

Finish machine tall vertical walls with shorter tool

Drawings

Cimatron has the capabilities for producing detailed and assembly drawings. For example:

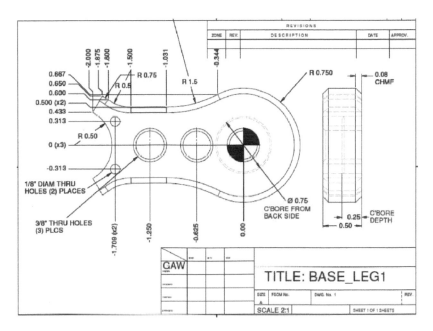

Detailed drawing

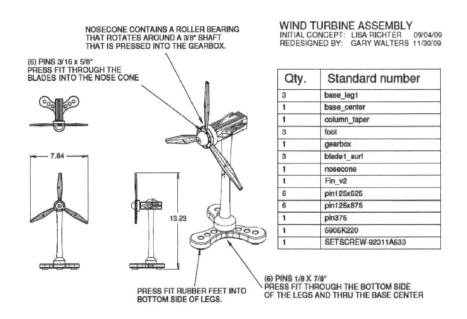

Assembly drawing complete with BOM (Bill of Materials)

Assembly

Cimatron has the capability of creating assemblies. This allows for simultaneous— or concurrent—engineering. Each part document can be assembled into a complete object.

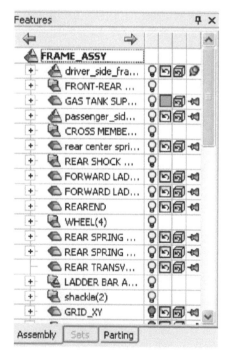

This car was assembled from multiple part documents, such as the gas tank, crossmember, wheels, ladder bars, etc.

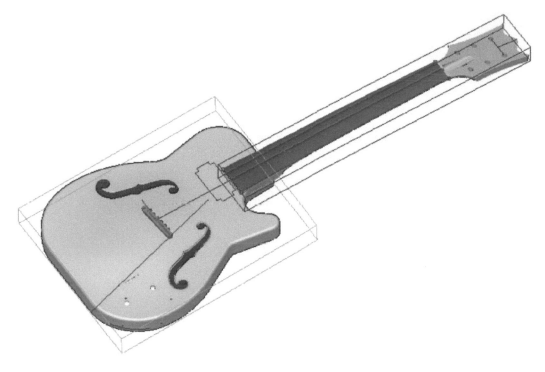

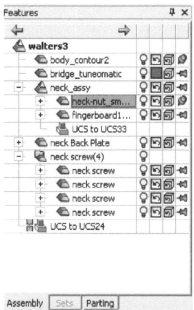

This guitar was assembled from multiple part documents, such as the body, bridge neck, etc.

Chapter 2: Navigating the User Interface

Screen Layout

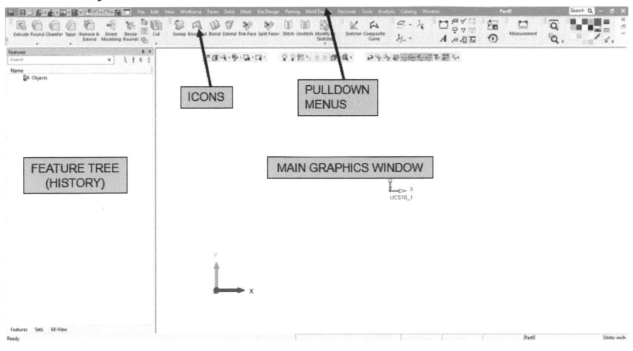

The screen layout contains a lot of action. So rather than describing everything at the start, let's focus on what you'll need to get started. 80% of the functions are advanced and we may never use them.

The top row consists of pulldown menus—easily readable in English. These menus equate to the **icons in the 2nd row**. I prefer to use readable menus when starting out, but it takes more menu picking to get to the final selection. As you progress, you'll prefer icons, as functions can be executed in just one click.

File

The File menu looks cumbersome. So as a beginner, we'll focus only on the basics. For now you need to know how to **create new part documents** (files) and how to **open previously saved part documents** (files).

Select **File** from the far-left pull-down menu:

To start a **new** part document in **INCH** mode, select the **Part_Inch** icon located in the top-left corner of the window.

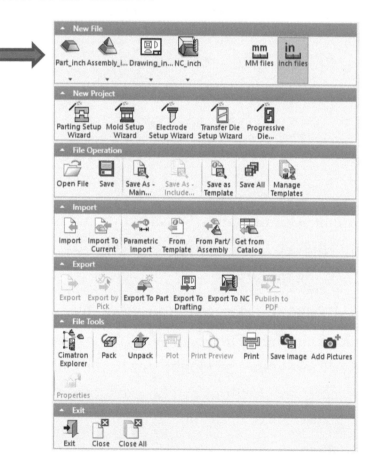

To open a previously saved Cimatron part document, select the **Open File** icon located midway down on the left.

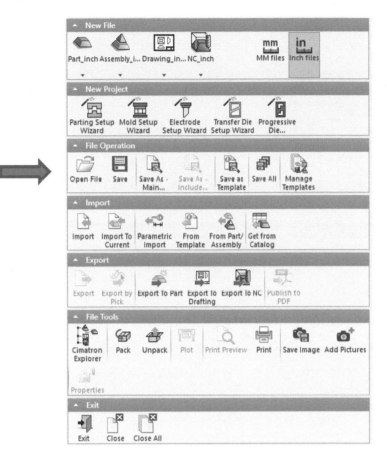

Help

The Help menu can be found under the **Window** menu. It can also be accessed by pressing the **F1** function key at any time. Help is context sensitive, so it will attempt to offer help pertaining to the current function you're accessing.

Cimatron also contains built-in **tutorials** for learning how to design parts, molds, program toolpaths, and more. Most of them are a bit advanced at this stage, so I recommend following this book to get started. We may revisit them later.

System Prompt

The system prompt is always located in the lower-left corner of the screen. For every function you select, there will be a prompt assisting you along the way.

Example 1, when defining a sketch, Cimatron wants to know which plane you wish to create a new sketch on. Therefore, it displays the following prompt in the lower-left corner of the screen:

Pick entities to define the plane.

Example 2, when defining a rectangular shape in the sketcher, Cimatron wants to know where to start the first corner. Therefore, it displays the following prompt in the lower-left corner of the screen:

Pick the rectangle start corner.

Note: It's common to see the following prompt when selecting entities to move, delete, copy, change color, etc. To accomplish the task, select the entities, then press your **middle mouse button** (MB2). The middle mouse button is what Cimatron refers to as **exit**, or completing the function.

Pick the entities and then <exit>.

Entity Selection:

Entities refers to anything created in CAD, such as lines, arcs, and circles, as well as dimensions, text, etc. Sometimes it's necessary to select entities in order to perform certain operations, such as copy, move, delete, change color, etc.

Entity selection can be performed many ways, but to start out, we'll keep it simple and basic.

Method 1: Pick the object with your left mouse button (MB1). It will highlight (change color) and remain highlighted until you cancel it.

Method 2: Using your left mouse button, press and hold while dragging a window around the object. It can be a partial window or full window. It will highlight (change color) and remain highlighted until you cancel it.

Entity Deselection:

Sometimes it's necessary to deselect entities.

Method 1: To deselect everything, select the red X as shown below:

Method 2: Select each entity one by one with your left mouse button (MB1).

Redo/Undo

Like most CAD systems, Cimatron offers the ability to "**undo**" the last operation performed. It can used multiple times to go back in time.

REDO is used to cancel the effect of undo. In other words, let's say you created a Taper feature. Then you select Undo to cancel it. But then you decided you really did want it! Redo will bring back the taper. Confusing? Yes, you won't use Redo on a regular basis.

These functions can be found in the top row of the layout:

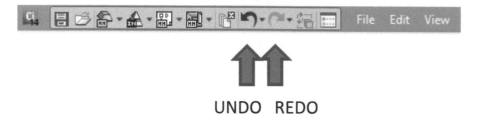

UNDO   REDO

Alternative to selecting the Undo icon, you can press **Control-Z**. This is a universal Windows function that works in many systems.

Feature Guide

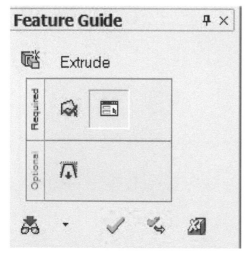

The feature guide displays in the top-left corner of your screen every time you perform a function. It allows you select options before completing the function.

Hovering your mouse over each icon reveals their function. The options change from function to function, but the following three icons are always the same:

Staring from right-to-left:

- The **yellow X** allows you to cancel (abort) the function.
- The **small green checkmark** serves as an Apply button. Just like Windows, pressing the small green checkmark performs the desired function and *remains* in the function, allowing you to create another feature right away.
- The **large green checkmark** serves as the OK button. Just like Windows, pressing the large green checkmark performs the desired function and *exits* the function.
- The glasses icon in the far left corner serves as a Preview function. It allows you to preview the results of the function prior to applying it. Note: most functions are automatically previewed.

3 Button Mouse

Cimatron takes full advantage of a 3-button mouse. In fact, it's a requirement to run Cimatron efficiently.

In the descriptions below, we'll refer to mouse button 1 as MB1, mouse button 2 as MB2, and mouse button 3 as MV3. MB2 is usually a wheel that scrolls in and out. But it can also be pressed as a button.

MB1 is used to **select** things like geometry and menus. It's the natural selection method.

MB2 is used to **EXIT**. Exit is the term used by Cimatron to identify that you have completed your selections.

MB3 is used to select **submenus**. Clicking this button displays a variety of submenus depending upon the function you're within.

Various combination of buttons can be pressed simultaneously to perform special functions.

MB1 & MB2 pressed together serves as an UNDO function.

MB2 & MB3 pressed together presents a **View** menu containing functions such as Zoom In, Zoom by box, a variety of Rotate functions, and more.

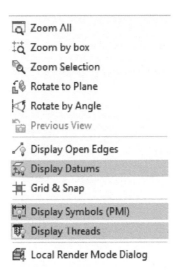

MB 1 & MB3 pressed together present a **Point Selection** menu. This menu allows you to specify how to select points. Notice DELTA option at the bottom. Ths allows you to input XYZ coordinates directly.

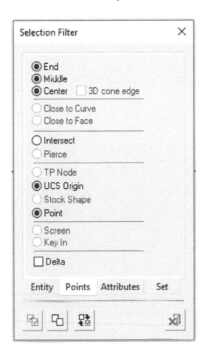

ZPR (Zoom, Pan, & Rotate)

One of the first things you need to learn when learning a new CAD application is how to **Zoom, Pan, and Rotate** the model. It's like driving a car for te first time and learning how to shift, or turn, or stop the car.

These functions are performed routinely as you develop more and more geometry and features. Sometimes you want to zoom for a closer look, then back out. You may wish to pan left or right. And often times you'll rotate the model in 3D to gain different perspectives.

There are different ways to zoom, pan, and rotate.

ZOOM:

1. Press and hold the **Control key** on your keyboard. Then press, hold, and move **MB3** to zoom in and out.

2. Select the icons from the top:

PAN:

1. Press and hold the **Control key** on your keyboard. Then press, hold, and move **MB2** to pan left-right and top-down.
2. Position your cursor to the sphere inside the User Coordinate System – located in the lower-left of the screen. Click on the left-right keys or up-down keys within the sphere.

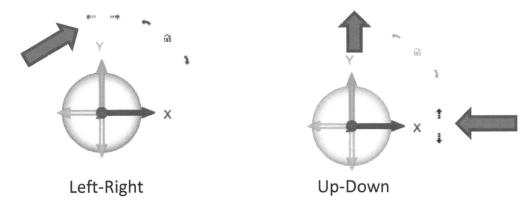

Left-Right   Up-Down

ROTATE:

1. Press and hold the **Control key** on your keyboard. Then press, hold, and move **MB1** to rotate.
2. Position your cursor to the sphere inside the User Coordinate System – located in the lower-left of the screen. Press, hold, and rotate MB1 within the sphere.

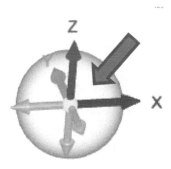

UCS (User Coordinate System

By default there is only one UCS, and it's prenamed **MODEL**. But you can create as many user coordinate systems as you like. However, only one UCS is *active* at a time.

UCSs are created by selecting the icon on the top row. When selecting the *arrowhead* in the icon, the following options appear for definition:

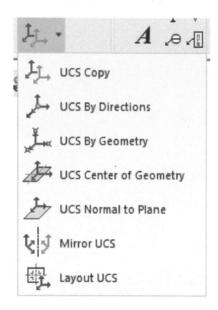

UCS's are useful when designing on different planes. They are also useful for creating multiple setups when CNC programming. For example, you may wish to have one UCS in the top-center of a part to machine from the top side. Then you may wish to have another UCS on the side of the part to tip the part on the machine and machine from the side.

On a typical one sided part, I define a user coordinate system in a location that will be used to define X0 Y0 Z0 on the CNC machine.

On a typical two sided part—one that will be machined from the top, then rotated to machine the bottom, I define two UCSs. They can be renamed to anything you like, too. So I define the first operation being performed—in this case the bottom—as OP10. Then I rename the top side as OP20.

All shops are different in how they locate X0 Y0 Z0. Some locate Z0 at the top of the part, while others locate it at the bottom—all for good reason. The exercises in this book places Z0 at the top of the part.

And X0 Y0 could be located at the top center of the part, or the lower-left corner, or at a dowel pin in a mold. In this book, we'll usually locate top-center.

UCS Manager

The UCS Manager is located in the ribbon near the top.

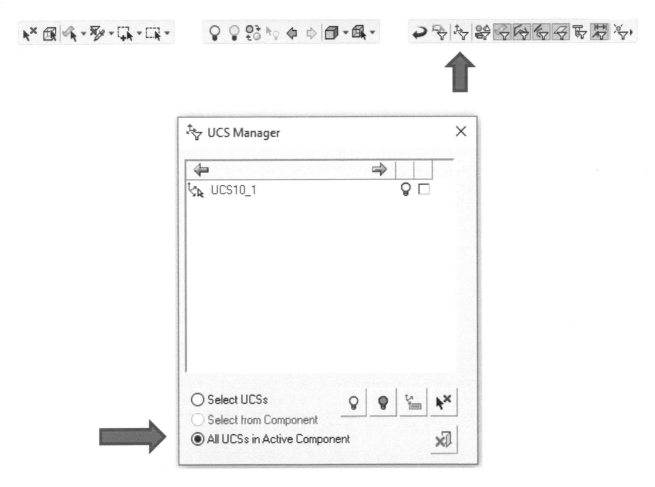

When you select "All UCSs in Active Component" all of the UCSs are displayed. In this example, there is only one UCS. It's named UCS10_1, which is the same as MODEL.

You can control **visibility** of the UCSs by turning the lightbulb on or off next to each UCS.

You can **rename** the UCS to something more meaningful, such as OP10 or OP20 for NC. This is accomplished by right-clicking on the UCS and selecting Rename.

You can **activate** a UCS in one of three ways:

1. Check the checkbox next to the lightbulb
2. Right-click on the UCS name and select Activate UCS
3. Close this panel (yellow x). Left-click the UCS in the graphics screen to activate. Then right-click and select Activate UCS from the submenu.

To activate a UCS, left click the UCS (to highlight it), then right-click and select Activate UCS from the submenu.

File Translators

Remember that the automotive companies in Detroit use Catia and NX. And that the defense industry uses Pro/E (Creaform). And the rest of the industries use whichever CAD system they choose...

Because not everything is designed in Cimatron, it must have the ability to import their files. This is done through a variety of means. The following file types are typical. Cimatron can import and export files by going through a translation process.

- **IGES**: International Graphics Exchange System. Useful for translating wireframe and surface only. It cannot support solid features.
- **SAT**: Useful for translating files that were created using the ACIS kernel
- **STEP**: Another common solid modeling translator
- **VDA**: This is European IGES translator, useful wh   en working with European customers.
- **Pro/E**: This allows for the direct importing of Pro/E (native) files.
- **Catia**: This allows for the direct importing of Catia (native) files.
- **NX**: This allows for the direct importing of NX (native) files.
- **Solidworks**: This allows for the direct importing of Solidworks (native) files.
- **Parasolid**: This allows for the importing of NX files.
- **DXF**: This is useful for importing and exporting flat 2D files. DXF is an Autodesk file format.
- **DWG**: This is useful for importing and exporting 3D files. DWG is an Autodesk file format.
- **STL**: Stereolithography format. This is a triangulated file type for exporting to Rapid Prototyping and FEM (Finite Element Modeling) systems.

Chapter 3: Introduction to Sketcher

Overview

Sketches are the underlying geometry used in solids. Sketches are used to develop extrusions, lofts, revolves, and much more. They are used in most CAD systems and work very similar. Once you learn the concepts of one sketcher, it's easy to learn another, such as Solidworks, Catia, etc.

Solid models are developed using a series of sketches. They start with an initial sketch. Then solid features are added or subtracted.

Rules

- **There can be more than one sketch.**
- **Only one sketch is active at a time.**
- **Sketches are planar**. The default planes are XY, YZ, and ZX. But you can define as many planes as you like to sketch on. When selecting te Sketch icon to create a sketch, Cimatron prompts you to select a plane to sketch on. Pressing MB2 (middle mouse button) chooses the XY plane of the currently active UCS.
- **Sketches can be open** when using them for CNC toolpaths, but not for solid modeling.

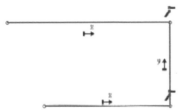

- **Sketches must be *closed* when using them to perform solid** functions. Their start and end points must coincide.

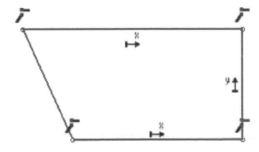

- Sketches cannot contain overlaps, intersections, or branches:

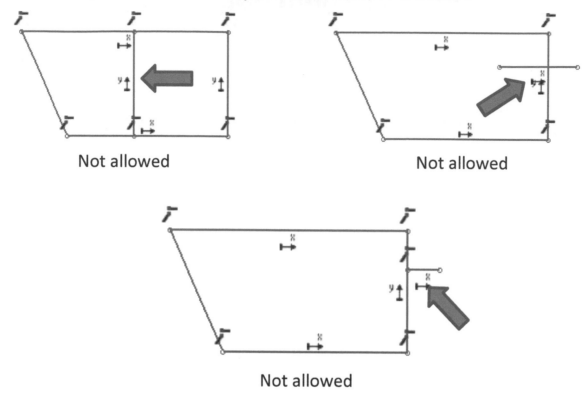

Not allowed   Not allowed

Not allowed

- **Sketches do not have to be dimensioned** to create a solid feature. Although before finalizing, it is strongly encouraged. ***NOTE***: some CAD systems require the sketch to be fully dimensioned before creating a solid.

- **Sketches can be drawn from scratch** using the tools within the sketcher. They include lines, rectangles, circles, splines, etc.

- **Sketches can be developed by referencing existing geometry.** When referencing existing geometry, the selected geometry is projected to the active sketch plane. This is useful when importing customer geometry and you want to guarantee building a model from it.

- **Sketches can reference other features** in the model (outside the current sketch). For example, it may be desirable to dimension a line in a sketch relative to a feature created from another sketch.

- **Sketches do not have to be constrained.** Although it is strongly encouraged before finalizing the project. Constraints include things such as angles, horizontal, vertical, coincident geometry, tangent, etc.

- **Sketches can be saved and exported for use in other documents.**

- **Sketches can be under constrained.**

- **Sketches cannot be over constrained.**

- **Sketches that are under defined remain dark blue.**

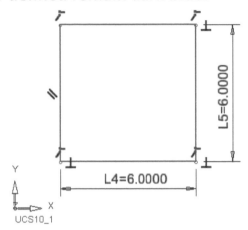

- **Sketches that are fully constrained and dimensioned (fully defined) turn purple.**

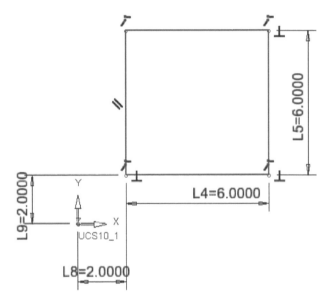

Constraints

Sketches contain ***constraints***. Constraints are used to constrain the geometry within the sketch. That is, lines can be constrained to horizontal or vertical. Two circles can be constrained to be share the same center point (concentric). A line and an arc may be constrained *tangent*. Two lines may be *parallel* or *perpendicular*. Two entities may share the same X or Y axis coordinate. And so on.

Constraint symbols appear next to each entity.

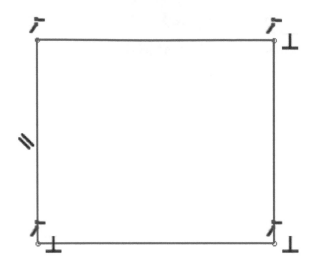

The top two constraints indicate that the line end points touch each other.

The left-most constraint indicates the left vertical line is parallel to the right vertical line.

The two constraints on the right and one at the bottom-left indicate the lines are perpendicular to each other.

Remember one of the rules above - sketches cannot be over constrained. Because the lines are perpendicular to each other, we're not allowed to create 90 degree dimensions between them. Cimatron will allow you to, but it'll flag it by drawing pale green dimension and brackets around the dimension [90.000]. When this happens, simply UNDO to avoid trouble downstream.

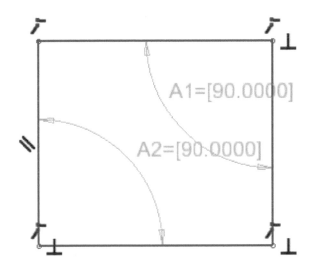

Constraint lines are useful when sketching. They assist you while sketching. For example, while creating a line, as it becomes more vertical, a constraint line appears. If you click on it, the line becomes true vertical. The same works for horizontal lines.

As the sketch grows, more and more constraints appear as you move your cursor around. Should you create a line that is nearly parallel to an existing line, you'll see a constraint. If you pick this constraint, the newly defined line becomes constrained and will be positioned parallel to the existing line. As you modify your sketch and the existing line moves, the parallel line will remain parallel.

Sketcher Tools

Although constraints assist you while sketching, be careful. Sometimes you don't want to constrain your geometry. To avoid constraining it, be careful not to pick on the constraint line.

But if you constrain something and wish to remove the constraint, you can select the **Tools** icon from the sketcher bar and delete it.

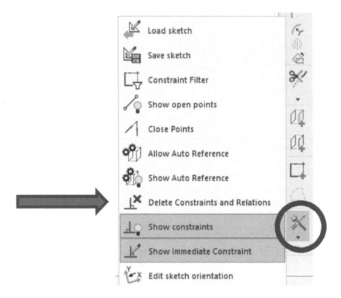

As the sketch grows—and there is more and more geometry—the constraints can get out of control. When this happens, they can be turned off by selecting the **Constraint Filter** from the Tools icon. Then you can check or uncheck constraints individually using this dialog.

Show Open Points:

A very useful feature in the **Tools** menu is the ability to find problems in your sketch. Remember from the rules above that gaps and overlaps are not allowed. But sometimes they're so small that the naked eye can't see them. So then how would you know these problems exist? You'll find out as soon as you attempt to perform a solids operation on it. If the sketch isn't closed and air tight, Cimatron will inform you and abort the operation.

When this happens, reopen the sketch and choose **Show Open Points** from the **Tools** menu.

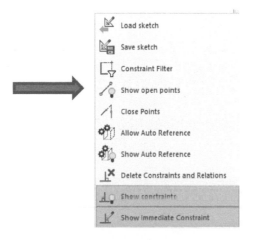

You can see by the example below that the geometry is untrimmed in the upper-right corner near the radius.

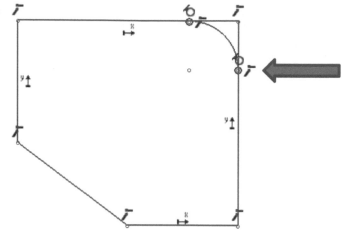

Problematic Sketch

Two red circles are drawn at the intersection of every problem. So no matter how complex your sketch becomes, these red circles jump out at you eye. To resolve the problem, zoom in close and observe. It's usually obvious. In this case, the CAD programmer forgot to trim away the corner geometry after creating the radius.

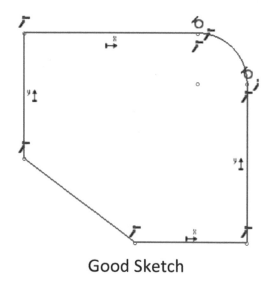

Good Sketch

Once the lines are trimmed, the circles disappear. Once again, this is an extremely powerful tool!

Chapter 4: Basic Sketcher Exercises

Sketch 1: Rectangle

This exercise teaches how to:

- Start a new part document in Inch mode
- Start a new sketch
- Define the plane to sketch on
- Create a 3 x 2 **rectangle**
- Dimension the rectangle and location of the sketch relative to X0 Y0
- Exit the sketch
- Save As a new part document

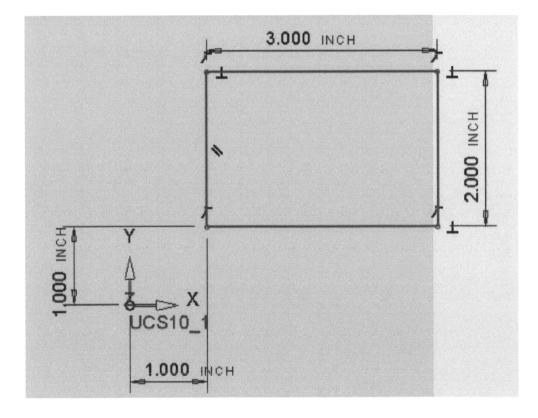

Sketch 2: Stepped Block

This exercise teaches how to:

- Start a new part document in Inch mode
- Start a new sketch
- Define the plane to sketch on
- Create a stepped block using **lines**
- Dimension the sketch and location of the sketch relative to X0 Y0
- Exit the sketch
- Save As a new part document

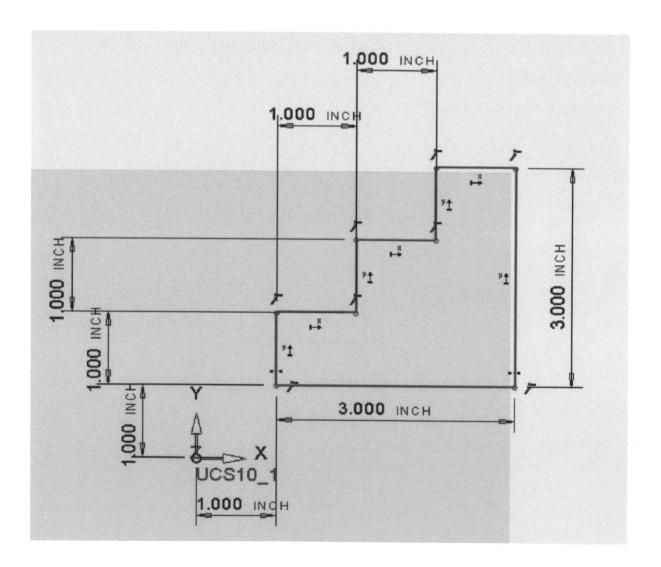

Sketch 3: Triangle

This exercise teaches how to:

- Start a new part document in Inch mode
- Start a new sketch
- Define the plane to sketch on
- Create a triangle using **lines**
- Dimension the sketch and location of the sketch relative to X0 Y0
- Exit the sketch
- Save As a new part document

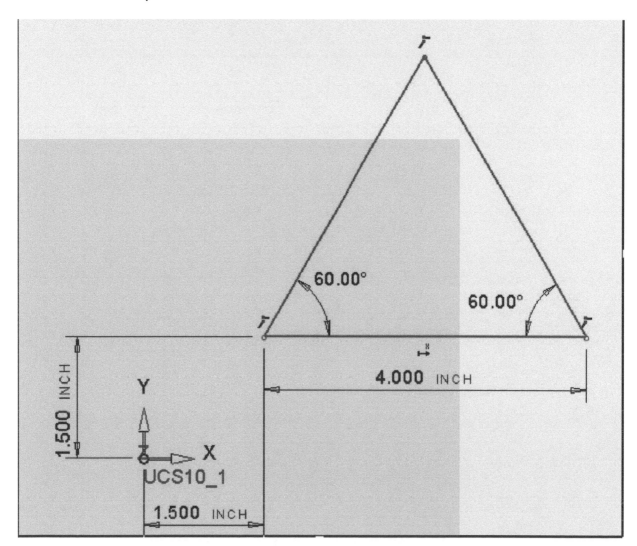

Sketch 4: Octagon

This exercise teaches how to:

- Start a new part document in Inch mode
- Start a new sketch
- Define the plane to sketch on
- Create an octagon using **lines**
- Dimension the sketch and location of the sketch relative to X0 Y0
- Exit the sketch
- Save As a new part document

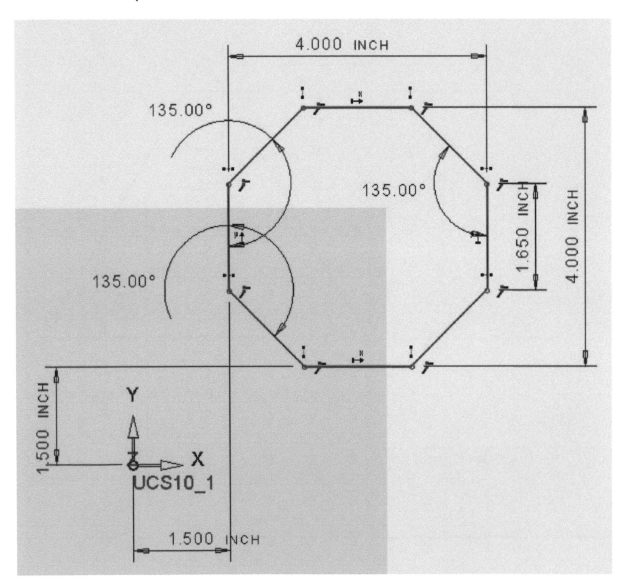

Sketch 5: Shape 1

This exercise teaches how to:

- Start a new part document in Inch mode
- Start a new sketch
- Define the plane to sketch on
- Create an object using **lines**
- Dimension the sketch and location of the sketch relative to X0 Y0
- Exit the sketch
- Save As a new part document

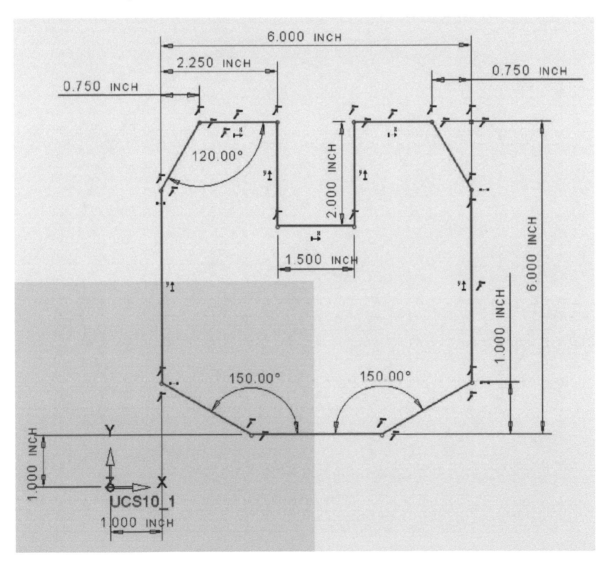

Sketch 6: Circle

This exercise teaches how to:

- Start a new part document in Inch mode
- Start a new sketch
- Define the plane to sketch on
- Create a circle using **Circles** using the UCS as the center point
- Dimension the circle
- Exit the sketch
- Save As a new part document

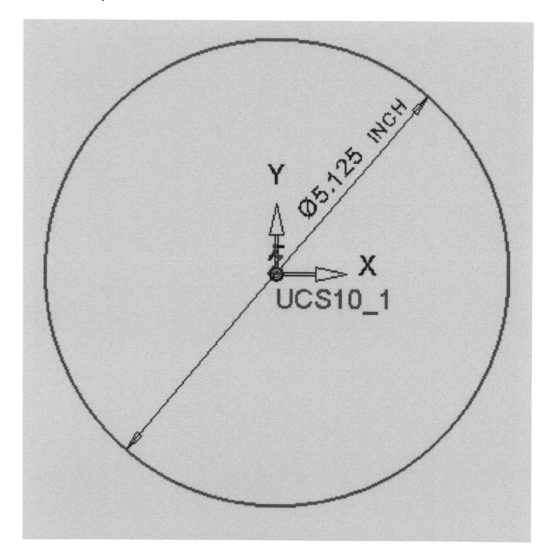

Sketch 7: Circle

This exercise teaches how to:

- Start a new part document in Inch mode
- Start a new sketch
- Define the plane to sketch on
- Create a circle using **Circles**
- Dimension the sketch and location of the sketch relative to X0 Y0
- Exit the sketch
- Save As a new part document

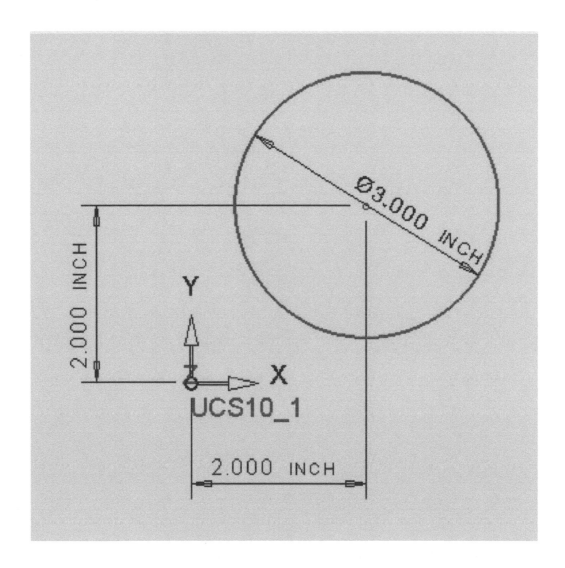

Sketch 8: Concentric Circles

This exercise teaches how to:

- Start a new part document in Inch mode
- Start a new sketch
- Define the plane to sketch on
- Create concentric circle using **Circles**
- Dimension the sketch and location of the sketch relative to X0 Y0
- Exit the sketch
- Save As a new part document

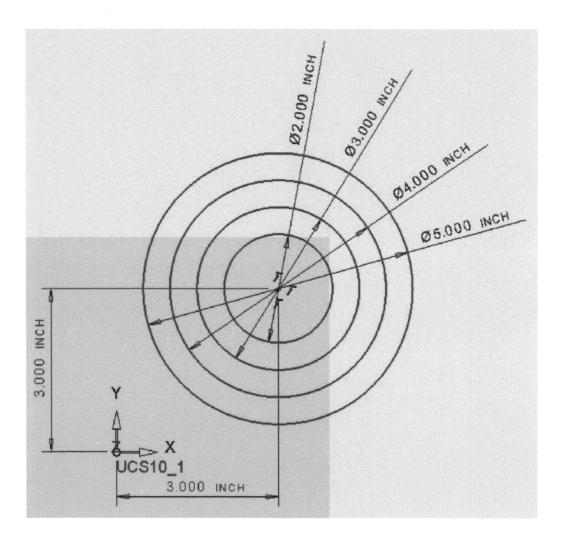

Sketch 9: Shape 2

This exercise teaches how to:

- Start a new part document in Inch mode
- Start a new sketch
- Define the plane to sketch on
- Create a part using **Circles and Lines**
- Dimension the sketch and location of the sketch relative to X0 Y0
- Exit the sketch
- Save As a new part document

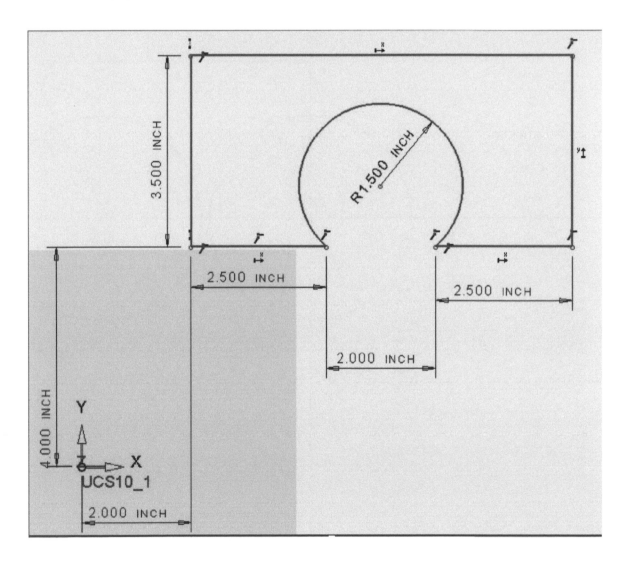

Sketch 10: Two Circles

This exercise teaches how to:

- Start a new part document in Inch mode
- Start a new sketch
- Define the plane to sketch on
- Create two circles sharing the same Y-axis
- Dimension the sketch and location of the sketch relative to X0 Y0
- Exit the sketch
- Save As a new part document

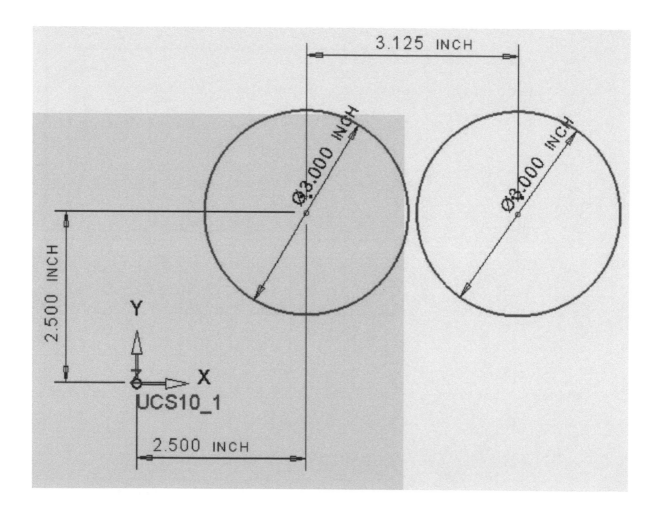

Sketch 11: Circles & Lines

This exercise teaches how to:

- Start a new part document in Inch mode
- Start a new sketch
- Define the plane to sketch on
- Create two circles sharing the same Y-axis, connected with tangent lines
- Dimension the sketch and location of the sketch relative to X0 Y0
- Exit the sketch
- Save As a new part document

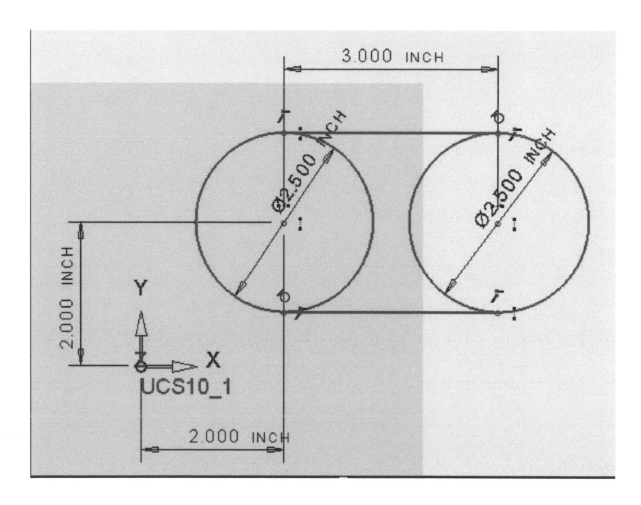

Sketch 12: Tangent Lines

This exercise teaches how to:

- Start a new part document in Inch mode
- Start a new sketch
- Define the plane to sketch on
- Create two circles sharing the same Y-axis, connected with tangent lines
- Dimension the sketch and location of the sketch relative to X0 Y0
- Exit the sketch
- Save As a new part document

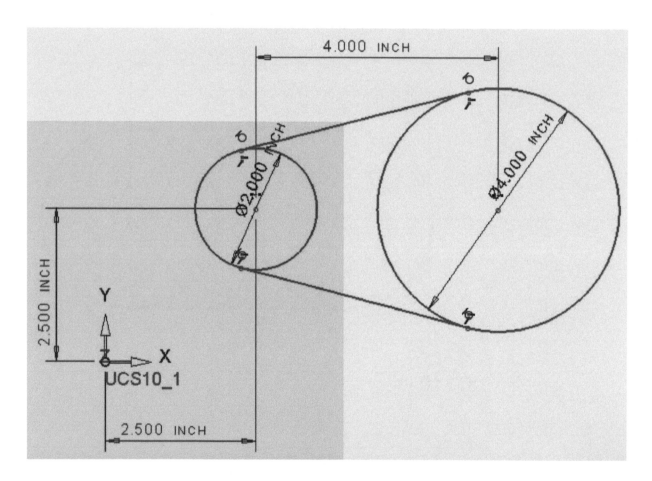

Sketch 13: Circles and Tangent Lines

This exercise teaches how to:

- Start a new part document in Inch mode
- Start a new sketch
- Define the plane to sketch on
- Create four circles connected with tangent lines
- Dimension the sketch and location of the sketch relative to X0 Y0
- Exit the sketch
- Save As a new part document

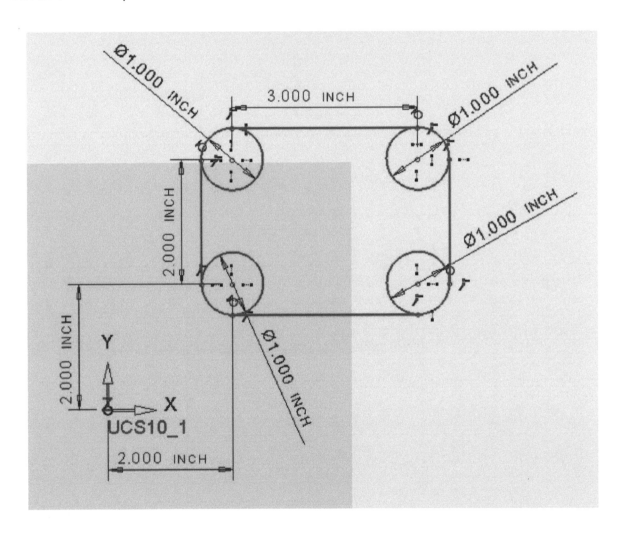

Sketch 14: Trim 1

This exercise teaches how to:

- Start a new part document in Inch mode
- Start a new sketch
- Define the plane to sketch on
- Create three circles connected with tangent lines
- **Trim** excess geometry
- Dimension the sketch and location of the sketch relative to X0 Y0
- Exit the sketch
- Save As a new part document

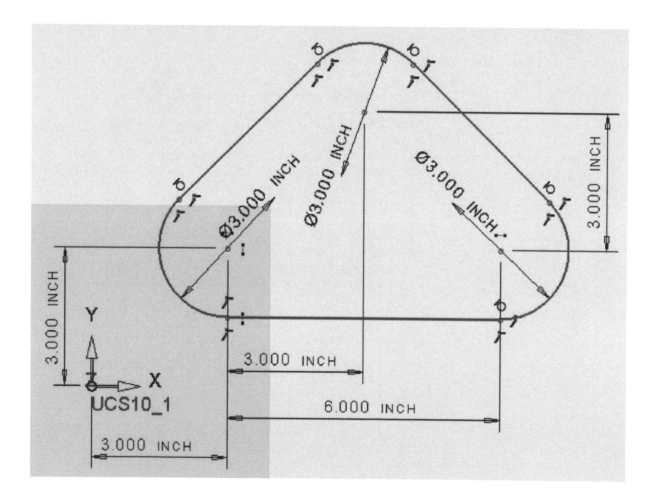

Sketch 15: Trim 2

This exercise teaches how to:

- Start a new part document in Inch mode
- Start a new sketch
- Define the plane to sketch on
- Create four circles connected with tangent lines
- **Trim** excess geometry
- Dimension the sketch and location of the sketch relative to X0 Y0
- Exit the sketch
- Save As a new part document

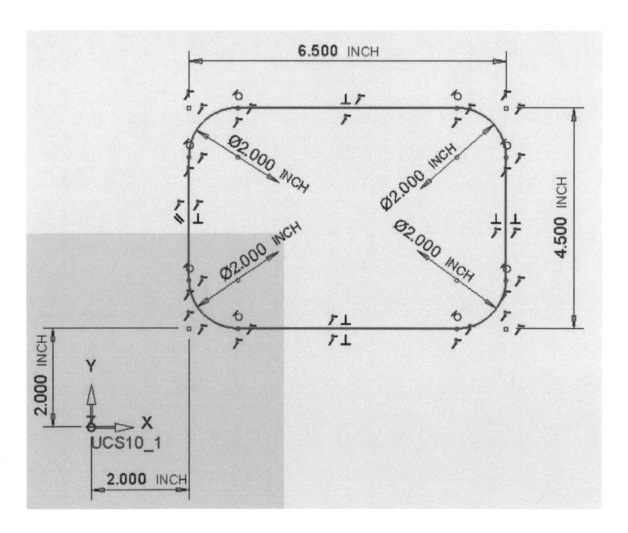

Sketch 16: Trim 3

This exercise teaches how to:

- Start a new part document in Inch mode
- Start a new sketch
- Define the plane to sketch on
- Create circles connected with tangent lines
- **Trim** excess geometry
- Dimension the sketch and location of the sketch relative to X0 Y0
- Exit the sketch
- Save As a new part document

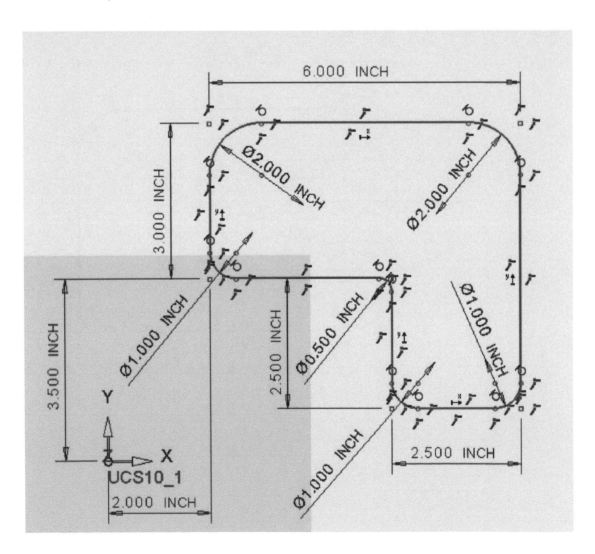

Sketch 17: Reference Geometry

Many time it's necessary to create a new *sketch entity* relative to an existing feature—from another sketch, or to *dimension* something relative to an existing feature—from another sketch. This is made possible by utilizing the "**Add Reference**" functionality in the sketcher tools pallet.

- Create a new sketch
- Close the sketch
- Create a solid extrude feature
- Create a second sketch
- Reference geometry from the first solid extrude feature

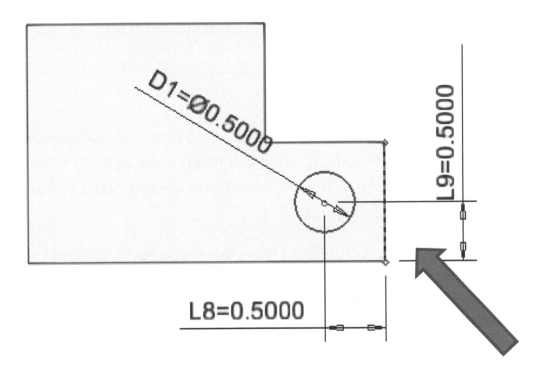

The large arrow on the right points at the reference feature picked from the solid feature to dimension the ½" circle from.

When picking a reference line, you are provided with two end points and a line from which you can construct new sketch entities.

Circles provide a center point, etc.

Sketch 18: Add Geometry

Many time it's desirable to create a *sketch entity* by picking an existing edge of a previously created feature. This is made possible by utilizing the "**Add Geometry**" functionality in the sketcher tools pallet.

- Create a new sketch
- Close the sketch
- Create a solid extrude feature
- Create a second sketch
- Add geometry from the first solid extrude feature to this second sketch

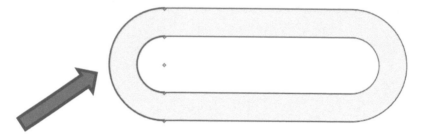

The two dark arcs shown on the left were selected from the **Add Geometry** menu. Unlike "Add Reference" where you can use the geometry to *build* from, this is *actual geometry* in the sketch. This is a very useful feature that ensures matching new geometry with existing geometry.

By adding two more lines to complete this sketch, you could achieve the following:

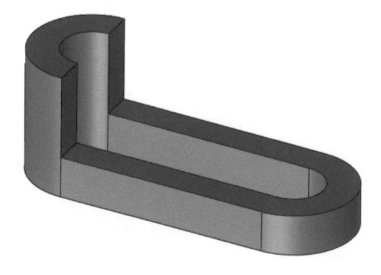

Sketch 19: Sketcher Quiz

It's finally time to put some of these exercises to test. On your own, create a new file and sketch the following. NOTE: the sketch should be purple upon completion.

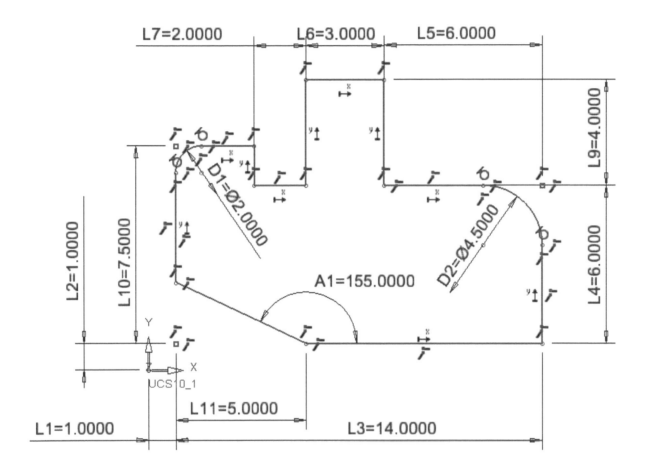

Chapter 5: Basic Solids Exercises

Extrude 1: NEW

This exercise teaches how to extrude a sketch to create a solid feature.

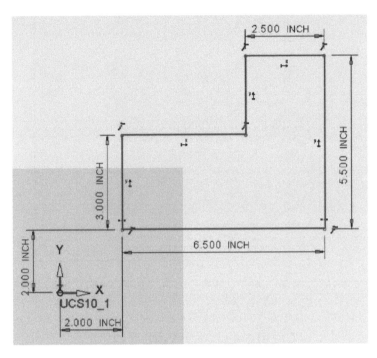

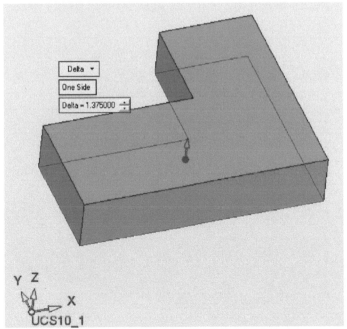

Extrude 2: REMOVE

This exercise teaches how to remove material with an extrude feature.

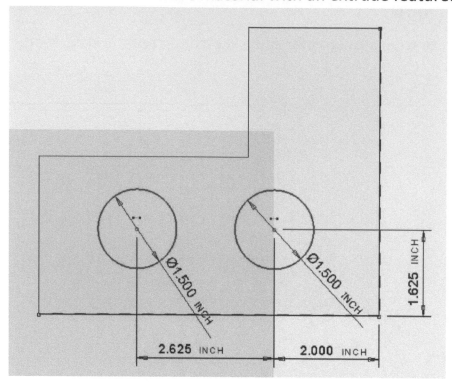

Create a sketch with 2 circles

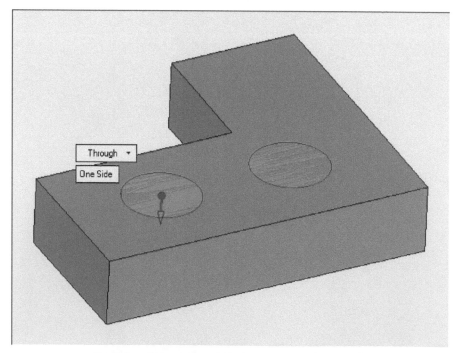

Solid > Extrude > Remove > Through

Modify Sketch

This exercise teaches how to modify the original sketch.

- Right-click on Extrude 13 in the feature tree.
- Edit Reference Feature
- Double-click the 7 dimension.
- Change it to 10 inches
- Select **OK** from the Feature Guide and exit the sketch.

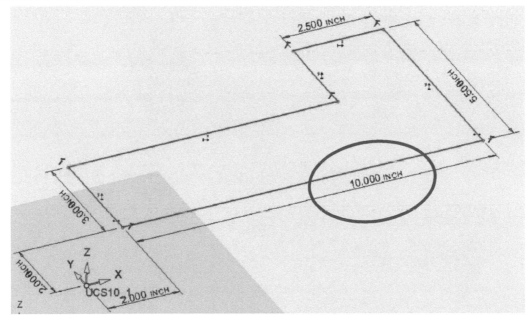

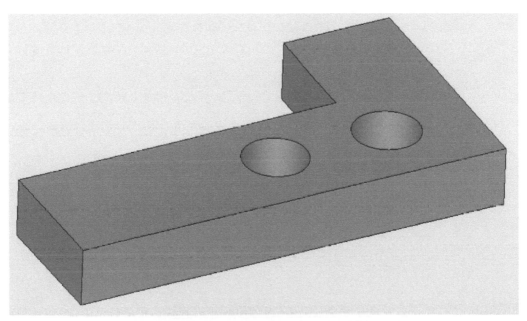

Final shape viewed in solids

Extrude 2: ADD

This exercise teaches how to add material with an extrude feature.

- Create a new sketch
- Pick the face shown below.
- Create the rectangular shape.
- Fully dimension it.
- Select OK from the Feature guide and exit the sketch.
- Solid > Add > Extrude > 0.5 inches

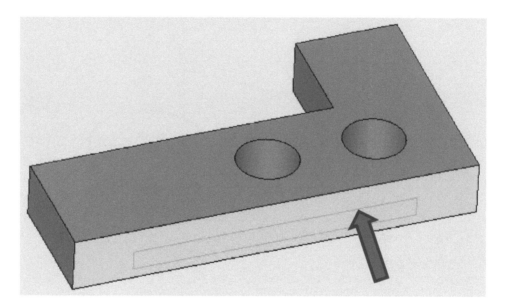

Pick this face to sketch on

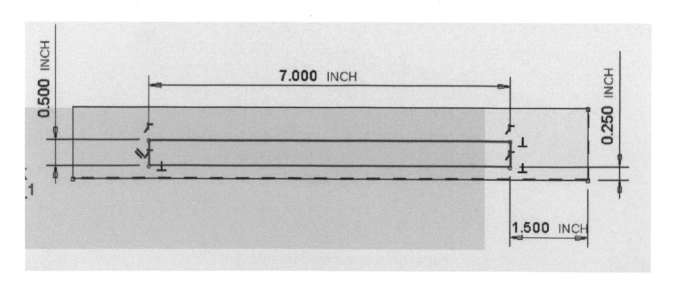

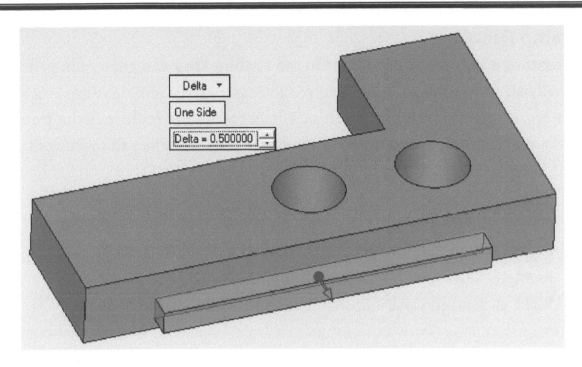

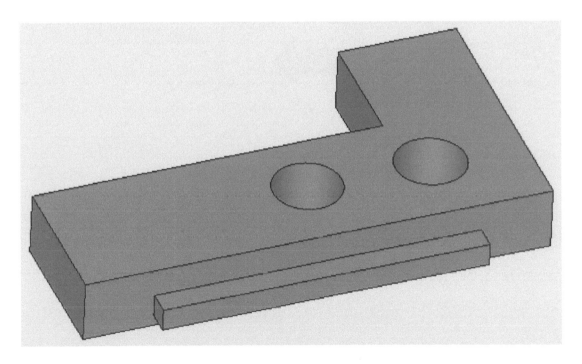

Completed solid

Rename Features

Each feature is automatically named in the Feature Tree. But their names reflect internally stored variables. As it becomes necessary to modify features, such as hole sizes, lengths of walls, tapers, it's difficult to find the feature in the tree. Therefore, it's strongly recommended to rename the features to make your model more friendly and easy to follow.

So in this model, I'd like you to perform the following:

- Right-click on the first feature and **Rename** it to MAIN BODY
- Right-click the next feature and **Rename** it to HOLES
- Right-click on the last feature and **Rename** it to SIDE RIB

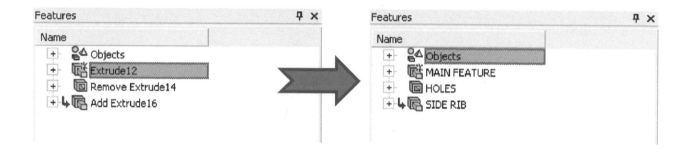

Rounds

Many models require rounded edges, or radii. Blueprint terminology specifies rounds are on outside edges and fillets are on the inside. But in Solids, we just refer to all of them as rounds.

- Solid > Rounds
- Pick the vertical corner edges and exit (middle mouse)
- Set the value to 0.5 inches
- Click OK from the Feature Guide

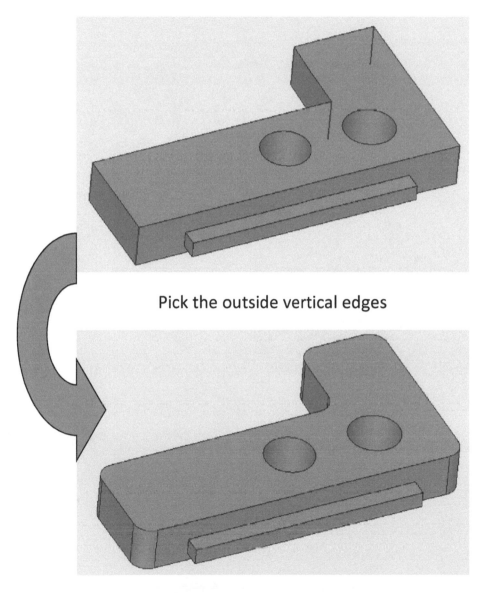

Pick the outside vertical edges

Completed model with rounds

Chamfers

Many models require chamfers along their edges. Many chamfers are 45 degrees, but some are not. 45 degree chamfers are referred to as symmetric. To change the angle to anything else, you simply pick the symmetric menu and add an angle.

- Solid > Chamfers
- Pick the top edge and exit (middle mouse)
- Set the value to 0.125 inches
- Click OK from the Feature Guide

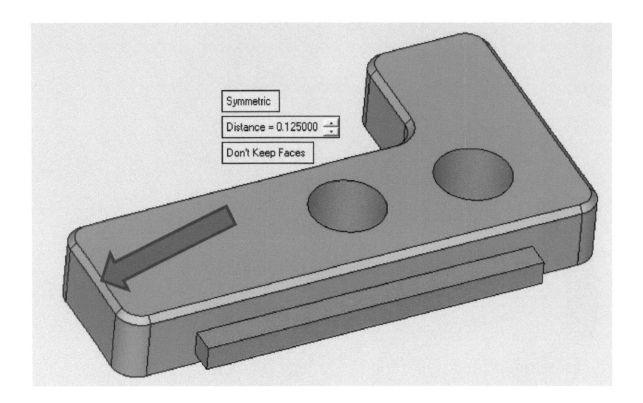

Shell

Molded plastic and sheet metal parts require wall thickness. This is accomplished by selecting a face to remove, and the rest of faces are given thickness.

- Solid > Shell
- Pick the bottom face and exit (middle mouse)
- Set the general thickness to 0.080 inches
- Click OK from the Feature Guide

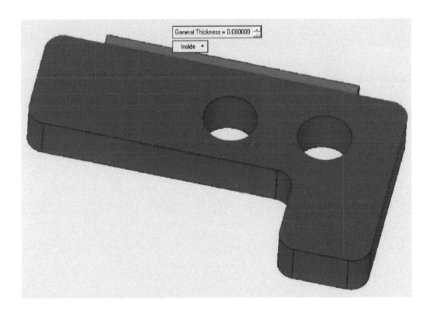

Pick bottom face

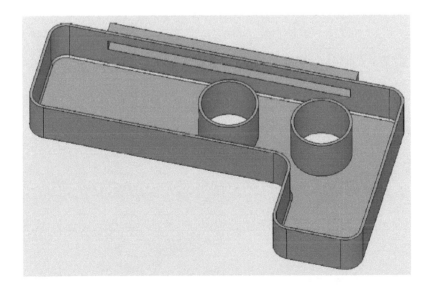

Completed shell

Feature Editing

Engineering changes are quite common in industry. This is why prototypes are usually made before the final product. Changes might include thickening the walls, changing a radius, moving a rib, adding more draft to walls, etc.

- Right-click on the round feature
- Select Edit Feature from the sub menu
- Change the global value to 1.25
- Click OK from the Feature Guide

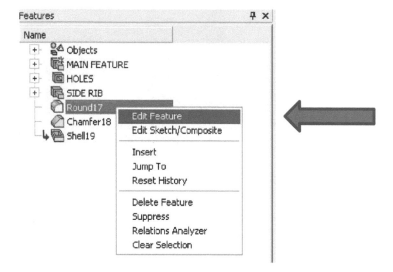

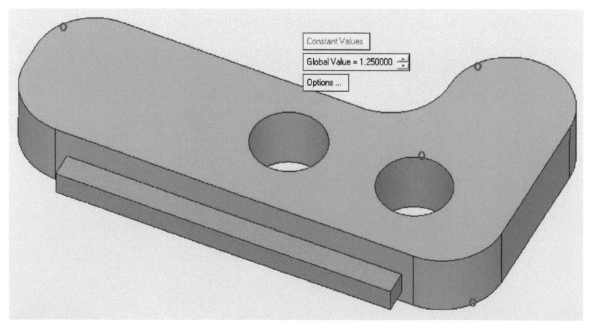

Solids Quiz

On your own, create a solid model starting with the sketch from the sketcher quiz, then add the following criteria:

- Extrude the sketch 2.375 inches
- Add 0.750 rounds to the three inside corners
- Add a 2.0 round to the lower right-hand corner
- Change the 12" long line along the bottom to 18.0 inches
- Shell the object 0.125 thick. Pick the top as the open face
- Add 0.125 Rounds to the 4 inside vertical edges
- Add 0.125 Round along the floor of the inside
- Edit the first extrude from 2.375 to 0.875

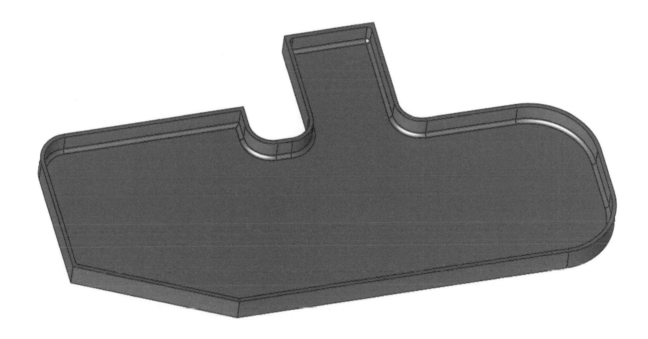

Chapter 6: Design Exercises

Design Exercise 1: Cardholder Base

Create three sketches and extrusions from the drawing below:

- Step 1: Sketch the outside rectangular shape, create a **new extrude**, then add the **rounds** to the corners
- Step 2: Sketch the inside pocket, then **remove extrude**
- Step 3: Sketch four points, then create counterbored **holes**

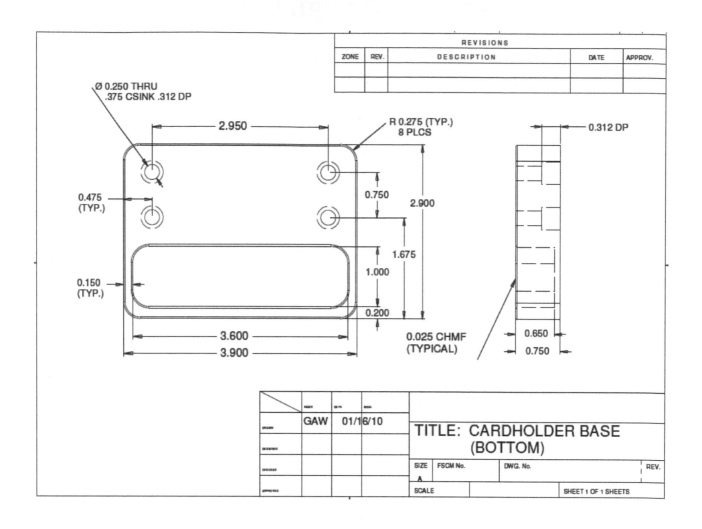

		REVISIONS		
ZONE	REV.	DESCRIPTION	DATE	APPROV.

Ø 0.250 THRU
.375 CSINK .312 DP

R 0.275 (TYP.)
8 PLCS

2.950
0.312 DP
0.475 (TYP.)
0.750
2.900
1.675
0.150 (TYP.)
1.000
0.200
3.600
3.900
0.025 CHMF (TYPICAL)
0.650
0.750

		NAME	DATE	BOOK	TITLE: CARDHOLDER BASE (BOTTOM)		
DRAWN		GAW	01/16/10				
DESIGNED							
CHECKED					SIZE A	FSCM No.	DWG. No.	REV.
APPROVED					SCALE		SHEET 1 OF 1 SHEETS

Start by creating a sketch of the outside rectangular shape. Anchor the lower left-hand corner 1 inch from the Model UCS in X and Y.

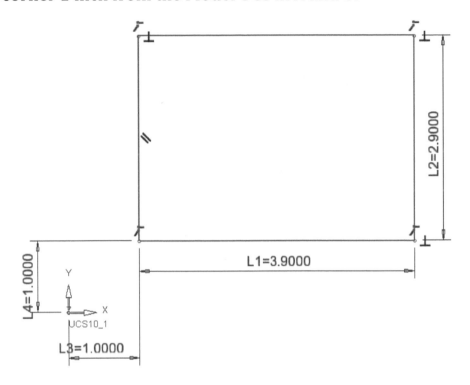

Exit the sketch and extrude it downward 0.750 inches.

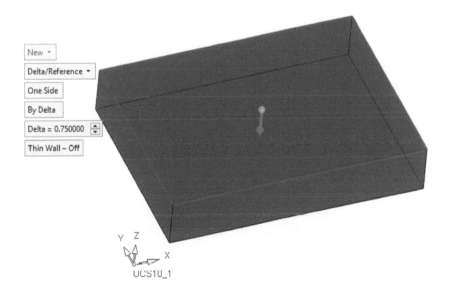

Add **0.275 Rounds** to the outside corners:

Rename the Features as follows:

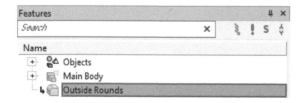

Create a second rectangular sketch on the top face. Add reference lines from the left and bottom edges to properly dimension the sketch.

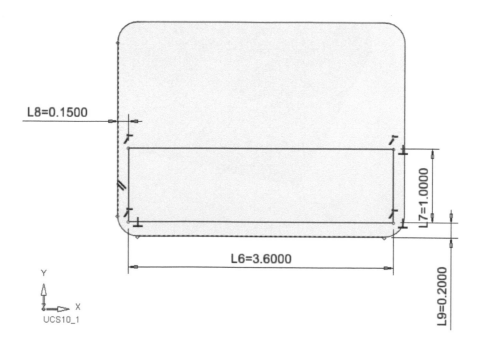

Exit the sketch and extrude - Remove it downward **0.650** inches.

Add the inside corner **0.275** rounds:

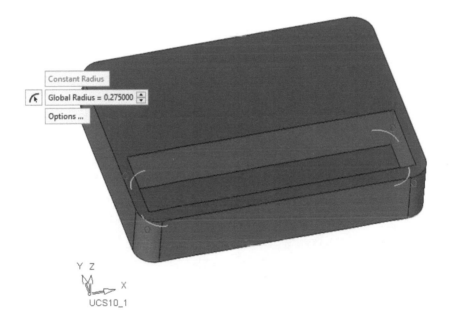

Create a third sketch from the bottom plane to locate the holes:

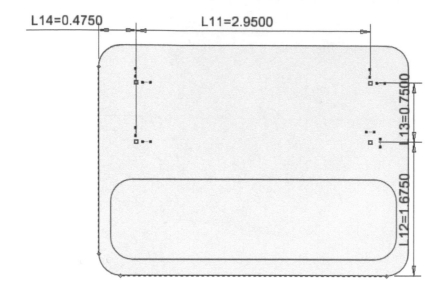

Exit the sketch and rotate the model such that it can be viewed from the bottom to watch as the counterbored holes as they're created.

Select **Solid** > **Hole**.

- Pick the four points. (They will become red when picked)
- **Middle Mouse** (Exit)
- Change Delta to **Through**
- Change **Diameter** to **0.250**
- Change Simple to **Counterbored**
- Change **Head Diameter** to **0.375**
- Change **Head Depth** to **0.312**

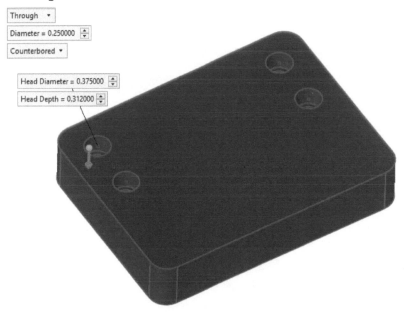

Press **OK** to complete the definition of the holes.

Rename the features as follows:

Completed Model:

Design Exercise 2: Mill301

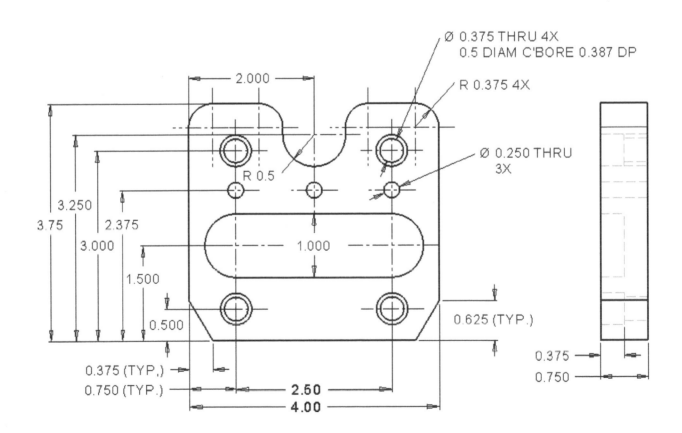

Start by creating a sketch of the outside rectangular shape. Anchor the lower left-hand corner 1 inch from the Model UCS in X and Y.

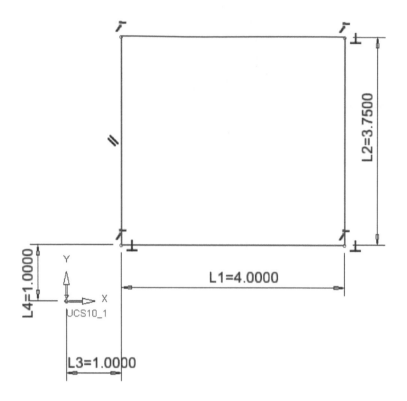

Sketch the **0.5 Radius** circle in the top center, followed by **two tangent vertical lines**. Do not dimension yet.

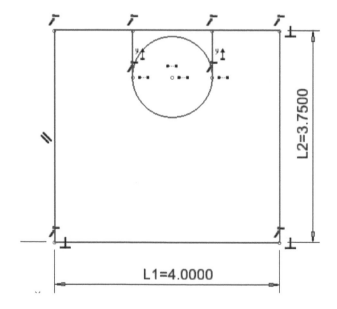

Trim the excess geometry and **dimension** the **location** of the circle, followed by the **diameter (1.0)**.

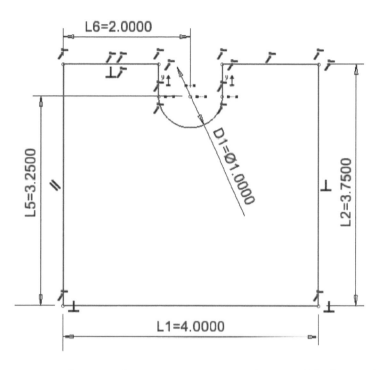

Sketch four tangent circles in the top corners. Then add their dimensions. The print calls for R0.375. But Cimatron may choose to dimension in diameter. Therefore, double the values.

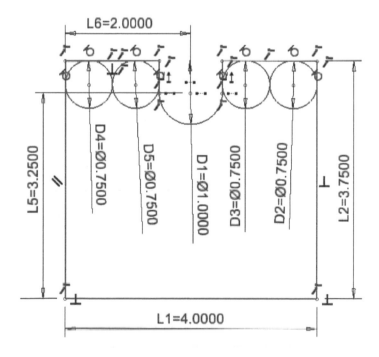

Carefully **Trim** the excess geometry, leaving only the radii. If you pick and trim the wrong entity once in awhile, simply UNDO. The easiest method for UNDO is to press the universal Control-Z on the keyboard.

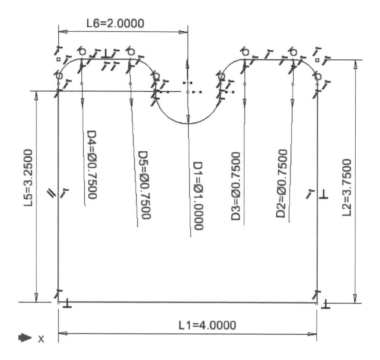

Sketch two chamfer lines in the bottom half of the part. Dimension them, and trim away the excess geometry.

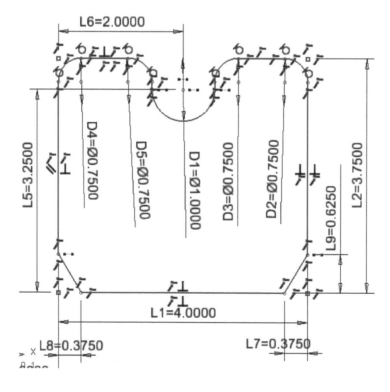

Exit the sketch and extrude it downward 0.750 inches downward, such that Z0 will be at the top of the part. Note: Since this is the first solid feature, it's automatically set to New.

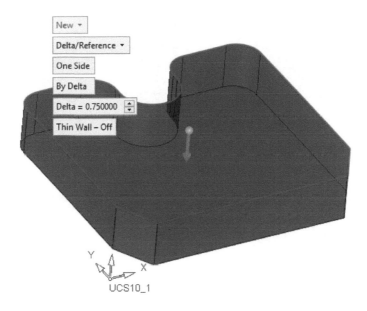

Create a second sketch on the top face of the part. Using circles and tangent lines, construct and trim the oval shaped pocket.

Add the outside vertical edges as **Reference** geometry to dimension the circles from the sides. Add the bottom horizontal as **Reference** geometry to dimension the circles from the bottom.

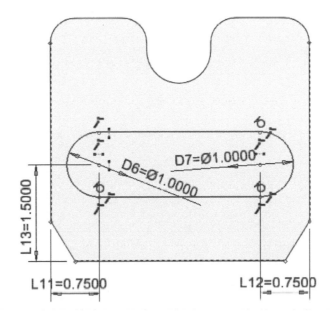

Exit the sketch and create another **Extrude.** This time, however, **Remove** the pocket **0.375 deep**.

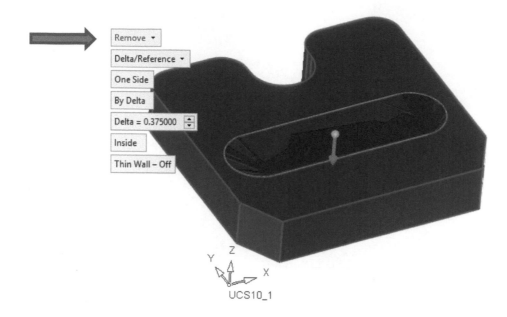

Create a third sketch on the top face of the part. Sketch and dimension three ¼" diameter holes.

NOTE: Using the **Add Reference** function, select the two circles from the pocket, and the top-center 1" diameter circle. Use these constraints to constrain the X-axis locations of all three circles. Then add the bottom horizontal edge to create the 2.375 dimension.

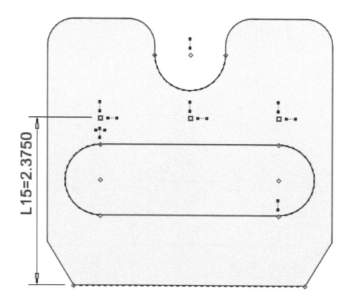

Exit the sketch. Select Solid > Hole. Pick the three point locations and exit (middle mouse button).

Change Delta to Through. And change the diameter to 0.250

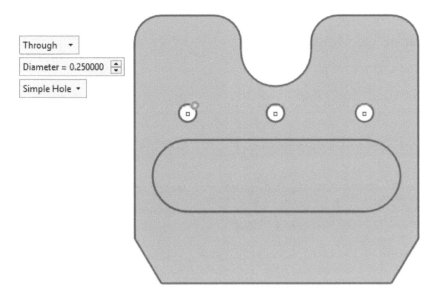

Select OK and create a fourth and final sketch from the top face.

Create four points to represent the counterbored holes. Add the two circles from the pocket as Reference entities to constrain the locations of the holes along the X-axis. Add the bottom horizontal edge as a Reference to dimension from in the Y-axis.

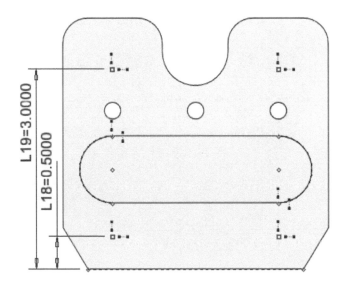

Exit the sketch and select Solid > Hole. Pick the four points and exit (middle mouse button).

- Change the Diameter to 0.375
- Change Simple to Counterbored
- Change the Head Diameter to 0.5
- Change the Head Depth to 0.387
- Pick OK from the Feature Guide

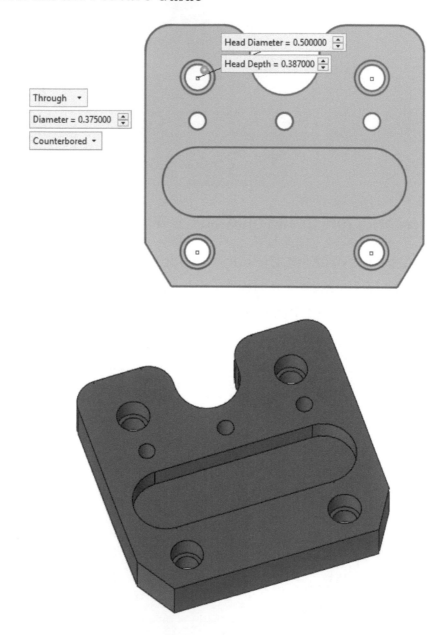

Rename the features and Save your work.

Design Exercise 3: Mill302

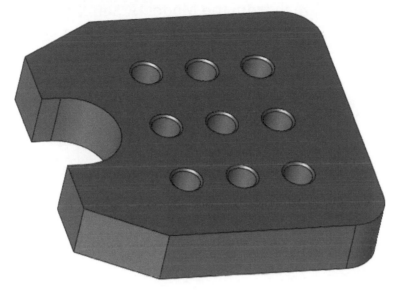

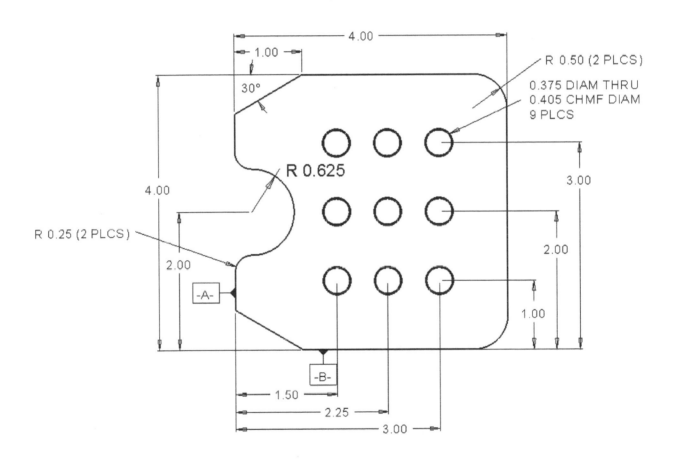

Start by creating a sketch of the outside 4x4 rectangular shape. Anchor the lower left-hand corner 1 inch from the Model UCS in X and Y.

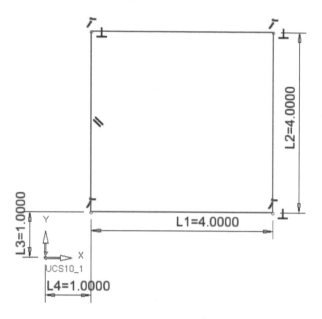

Create the **1.25 diameter circle** on the left (0.625 x 2).

Dimension the diameter of the circle, followed by the location along X and Y. *Note*: the 0.250 dimension was derived by extracting the radius of the R0.25 callout on the left (2 PLCS).

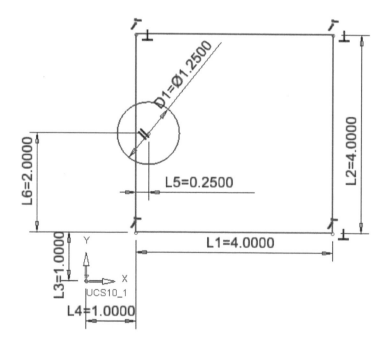

Create **two tangent lines**. I like to extend it a bit further than necessary and trim it back to ensure good horizontal lines. Of course, you don't have to.

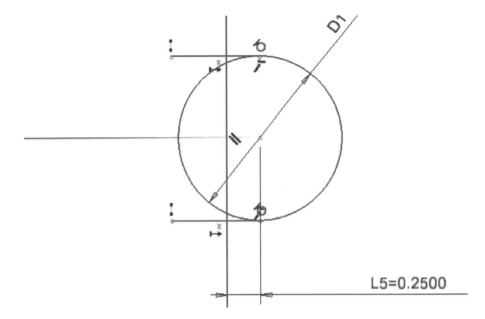

L5=0.2500

Trim all the unwanted segments.

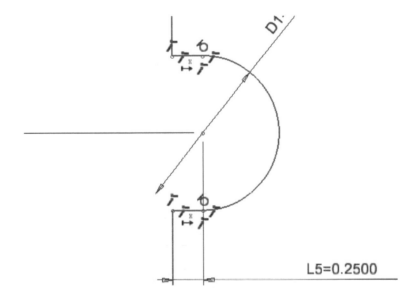

L5=0.2500

Extrude the sketch **0.750 upwards**.

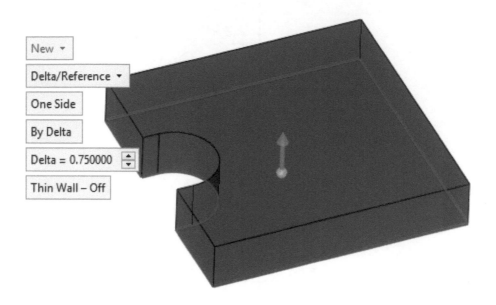

Create the two **0.500 corner radii**.

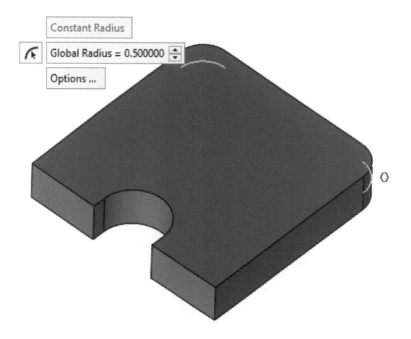

Create the **30 degree chamfer** in the top-left by picking the edge and pressing middle mouse (exit).

- Change Symmetric to **Distance- Angle**
- Change the angle to **30** degrees
- Change the distance to **1 inch**
- Press **Apply** from the Feature Guide

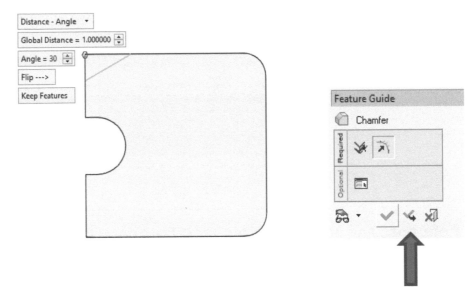

Pick the bottom left-hand corner edge to chamfer. Then press middle mouse (exit).

If necessary, press **Flip** to orient the 30 degrees properly. Then press **OK** from the Feature Guide.

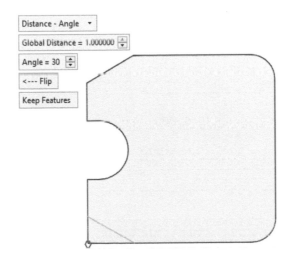

Create a new sketch on the top face and select **Points**. After creating the first point of nine, take advantage of the constraints to properly align the grid in X & Y.

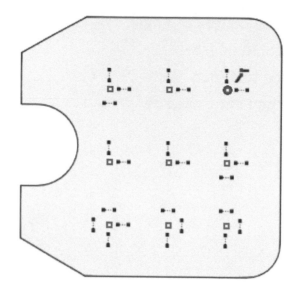

Select **Add Reference** and add the bottom-most horizontal line, followed by the left-most vertical line. These will be used to dimension the points from.

Dimension the points.

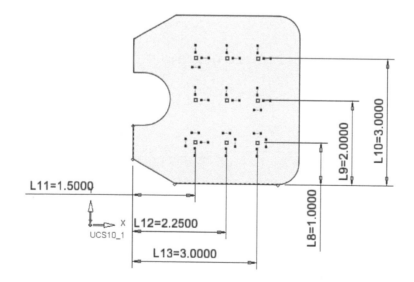

- Select from the Feature **OK** Guide.
- Create a **Solid – Hole** feature.
- Drag a window around the points—or pick them individually.
- **Middle mouse** (exit).
- Change Delta to **Through**
- Change the hole diameter to **0.375**
- **Press OK from the Feature Guide**

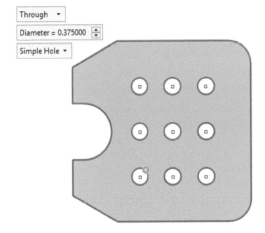

- Create a **Solid > Chamfer** feature.
- Rotate to an isometric view and pick the top edges of the holes—one at a time (total nine picks). *NOTE*: Window would grab too many features.
- Press middle mouse (exit)
- Change Distance – Angle to Symmetric
- Change the **Global Distance** to **0.030** (0.405 – 0.375)
- Press **Preview**, then **OK** from the Feature Guide

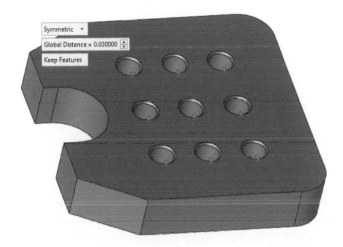

Design Exercise 4: NIMS210

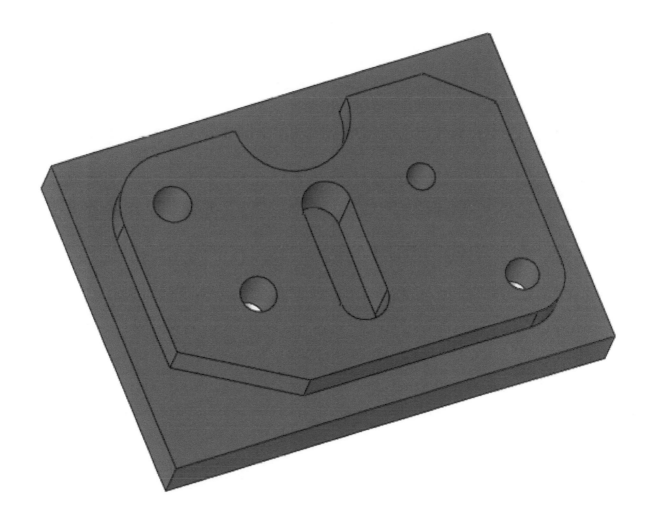

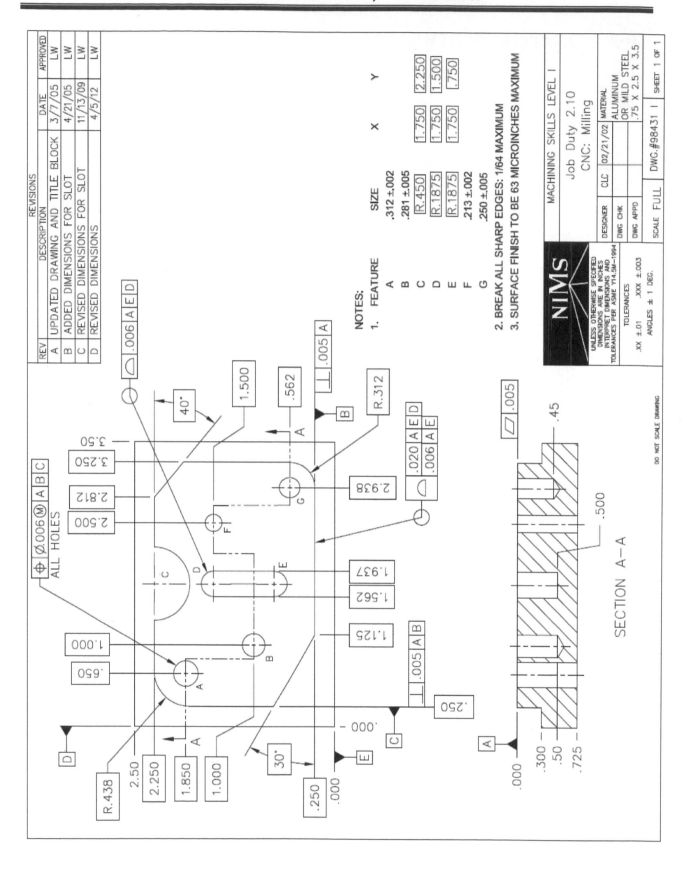

SECTION A-A

DO NOT SCALE DRAWING

Create a **3.5 x 2.5 rectangular sketch**. Anchor the sketch 1" away from the UCS by 1 inch in both directions.

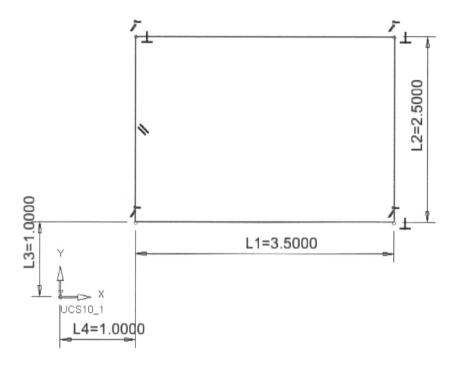

Extrude the sketch **0.425** upwards.

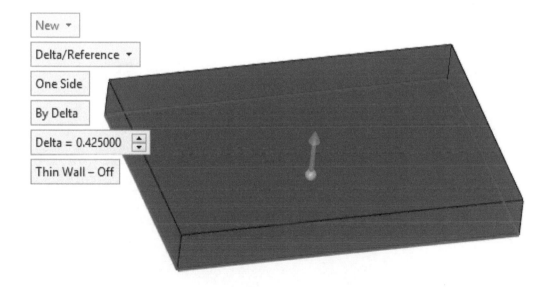

- Create a sketch on the top face.
- Select **Add Reference** and add the bottom-most horizontal line and the left-most vertical line.
- Sketch a **3 x 2 rectangle**.
- **Dimension** it as shown:

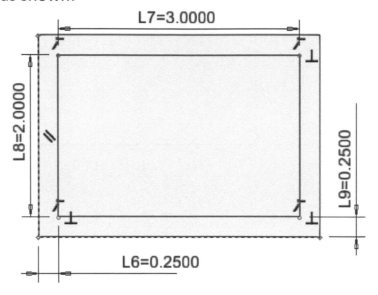

- **Extrude** the sketch **0.300** upward.

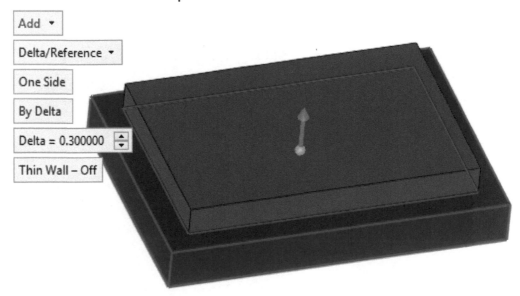

Create the **0.438 Round** feature in the top left-hand corner:

- Pick the vertical edge and **exit** (middle mouse).
- Change the radius to **.438**
- Press **Apply** from the Feature Guide.

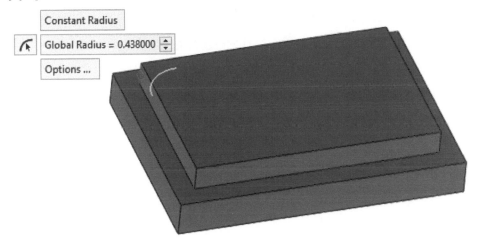

Create the **0.312 Round** feature in the bottom right-hand corner:

- Pick the vertical edge and **exit** (middle mouse).
- Change the radius to **.312**
- Press **OK** from the Feature Guide.

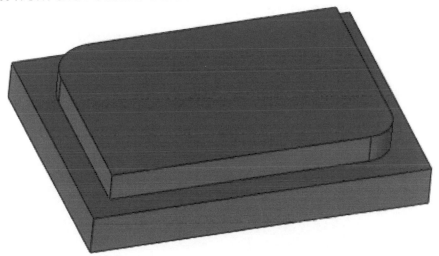

Select **Solid > Chamfer**.

- Pick the top right-hand corner. Then press middle mouse (exit)
- Change Symmetric to **Distance – Angle**
- Change the angle to **40** degrees
- Rotate to a plan view and zoom in closer around the corner
- Pick **Flip** to change orientation of the 40 degree angle
- Change the distance to **3.25 – 2.812**
- Select **Apply** from the Feature Guide

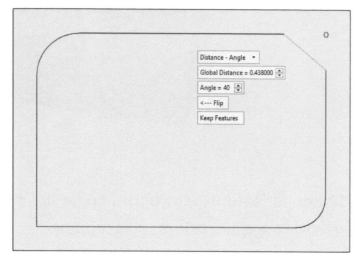

- Pick the lower left-hand corner. Then press middle mouse (exit)
- Change the angle to **30** degrees
- Rotate to a plan view and zoom in closer around the corner
- Change the distance to **1.125 – 0.250**
- Select **OK** from the Feature Guide

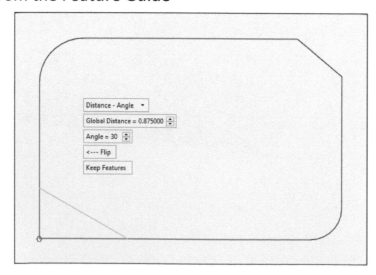

Create the top center 0.450 radius arc cutout:

- Create a new sketch on the top face.
- Select **Add Reference** and pick the **leftmost vertical line**, followed by the **topmost horizontal line** from the second sketch (**2.25 dimension**).
- Sketch a circle on the 2.25 line
- Dimension it: **0.9 diameter** (0.45 x 2)
- Create the **1.75** dimension form the left reference line
- Press **OK** from the Feature Guide.

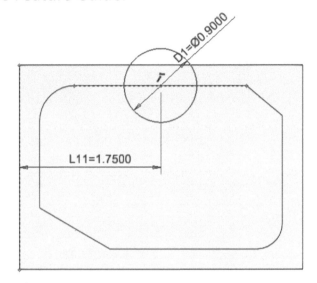

- Select **Solid > Extrude**.
- Change Add to **Remove**
- Change By Delta to **By Reference**
- Rotate the model so it can be viewed from the back
- Pick this face and press **OK** from the Feature Guide

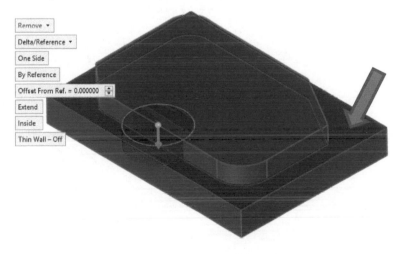

Create a sketch of the **through holes A and F**: Dimension their centers along X & Y

- Pick the top face to sketch on
- Sketch two circles and dimension them (A) 0.312 and (F) 0.213 diameters.
- Select Add Reference and choose the left-most vertical line, followed by the bottom-most horizontal line.
- Dimension their centers along X and Y.

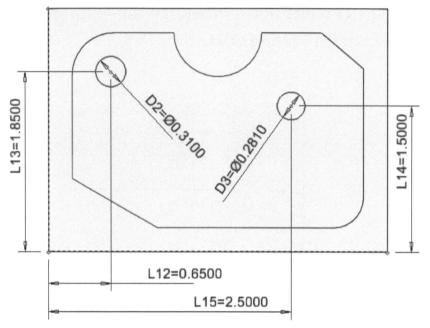

- Select **Solid > Extrude**
- Change Delta/Reference to **Through**
- Press **OK** from the Feature Guide

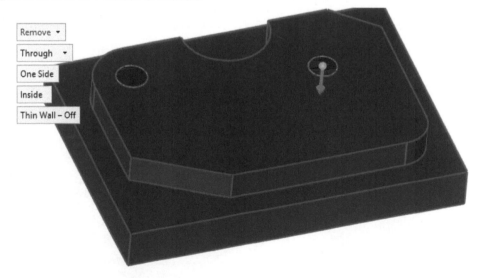

Create the **B hole**:

- Create a sketch on the top face
- Sketch a **point** in the approximate location.
- Select **Add Reference** and pick the left-most vertical line, followed by the bottom-most horizontal line
- **Dimension** the point along X and Y

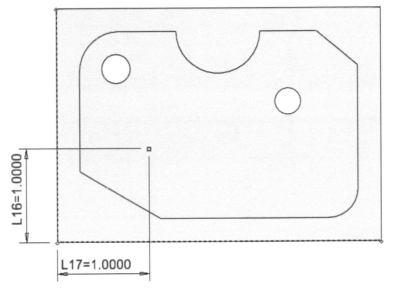

- Select **Solid > Hole**
- Pick the point and **middle mouse** (exit)
- Change Delta to **0.500 deep**
- Change the diameter to **0.281**
- Press **OK** from the Feature Guide

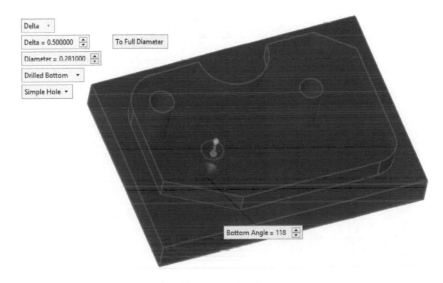

Create the **G hole**:

- Create a sketch on the top face
- Sketch a **point** in the approximate location.
- Select **Add Reference** and pick the left-most vertical line, followed by the bottom-most horizontal line
- **Dimension** the point along X and Y

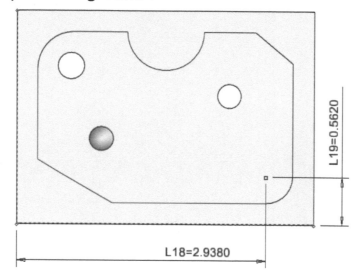

- Select **Solid > Hole**
- Pick the point and **middle mouse** (exit)
- Change Delta to **0.450 deep**
- Change the diameter to **0.250**
- Press **OK** from the Feature Guide

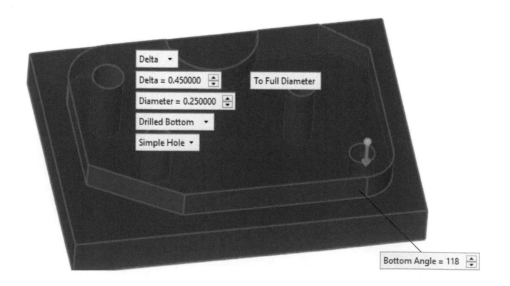

Create the vertical slot:

- Create a sketch on the top face
- Select Add Reference and add the top center 0.450 radius arc
- Sketch two circles as shown
- Dimension the circle diameters (0.375)
- Create two tangent vertical lines
- Trim away the unwanted entities
- Select Add Reference and pick the bottom-most horizontal line
- Dimension the Y locations of the slot

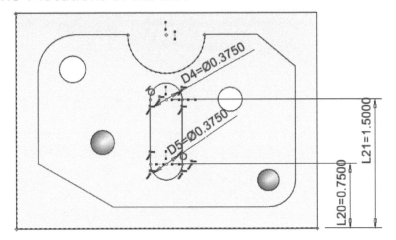

- Press **OK** from the Feature Guide
- Select **Solid > Extrude**
- Change Through to **Delta/Reference**
- Change By Reference to **By Delta**
- Change the depth to 0.500

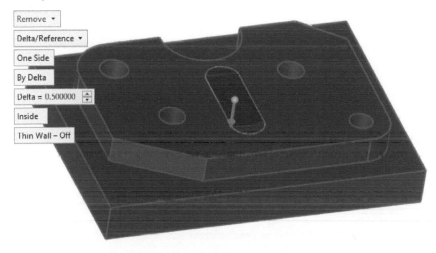

Press OK from the Feature Guide to complete this exercise.

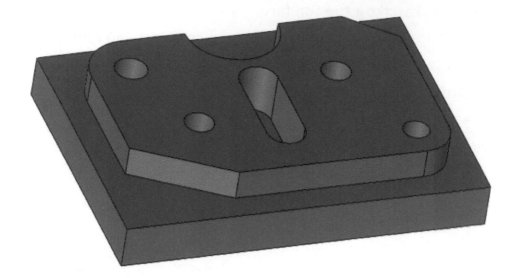

Design Exercise 5: 2400

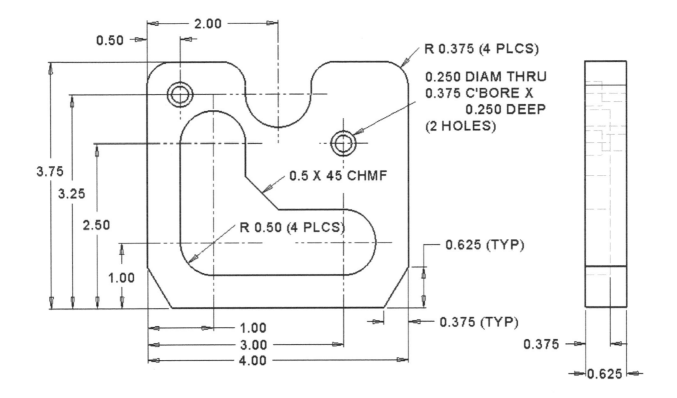

This outside shape of this part is the same as Mill302. Sketch the outside rectangular shape first. Then dimension it. Anchor the sketch 1" from the UCS.

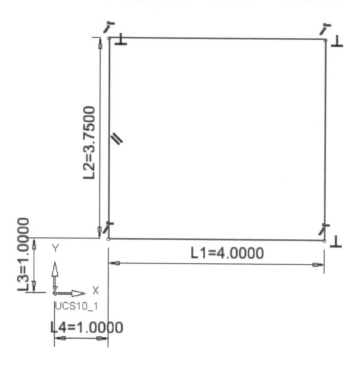

Sketch the top center 1" diameter circle and vertical tangent lines. Then dimension and trim.

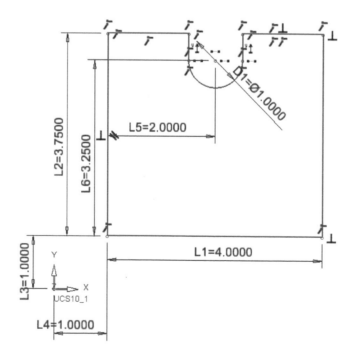

Sketch the four **0.375 radii** on the top corners, trim, and dimension. Remember that Cimatron wants to dimension circles in diameters, but the print calls them out as radii. So double your values.

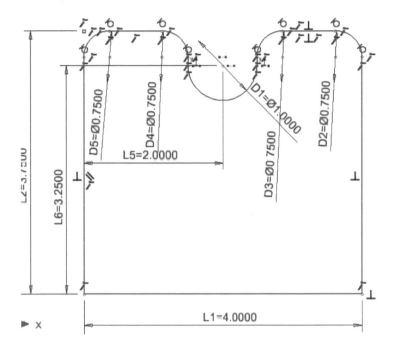

Exit the sketch (without chamfers) and **extrude** it **0.625** deep.

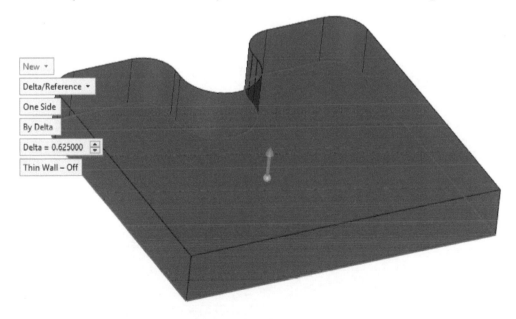

- Select **Solid > Chamfer**
- Rotate to an isometric so you can pick the vertical edge in the lower left-hand corner.
- Change Symmetric to **Distance – Distance**
- Add the values **0.625** and **0.375. Note:** you may have to reverse the numbers.
- Press **Apply** from the Feature Guide

- Rotate to an isometric so you can pick the vertical edge in the lower right-hand corner.
- Add the values **0.625** and **0.375 Note:** you may have to reverse the numbers.
- Press **OK** from the Feature Guide

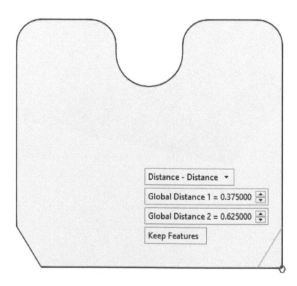

Sketch the inside pocket shape, trim, and dimension. I recommend starting with three 1" diameter circles. Then add tangent lines. Leave the chamfer out so we can add it as a solid feature later.

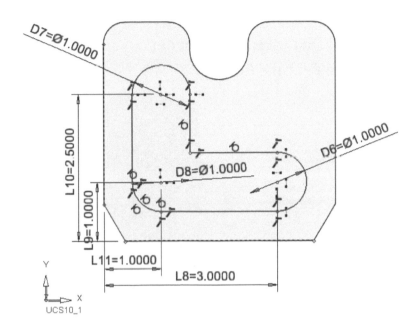

- Select **Solid > Extrude**
- Change Add to **Remove**
- Change Delta to **0.375**

- Select **Solid > Chamfer**
- In an isometric orientation, pick the vertical edge inside the pocket, then middle mouse (exit)
- Change Distance – Distance to **Symmetric**
- Change the Global Distance to **0.5** inches
- Press **OK** from the Feature Guide

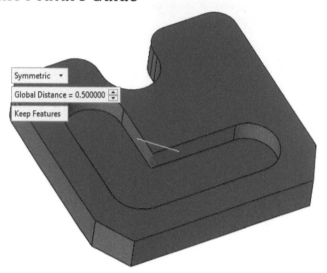

Sketch two point locations for the counterbored holes, then dimension. You'll need to add reference lines to dimension from.

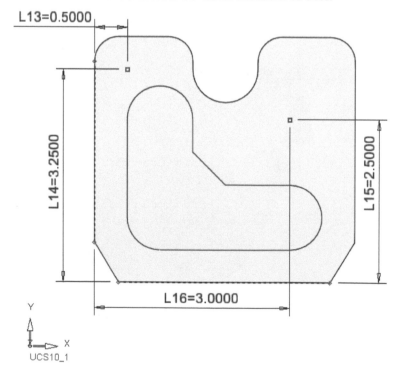

- Select **Solid > Hole**
- Pick the two points and press middle mouse (exit)
- Change Delta to **Through**
- Change diameter to **0.250**
- Change Simple to **Counterbored**
- Change Head Diameter to **0.375**
- Change Head Depth to **0.250**

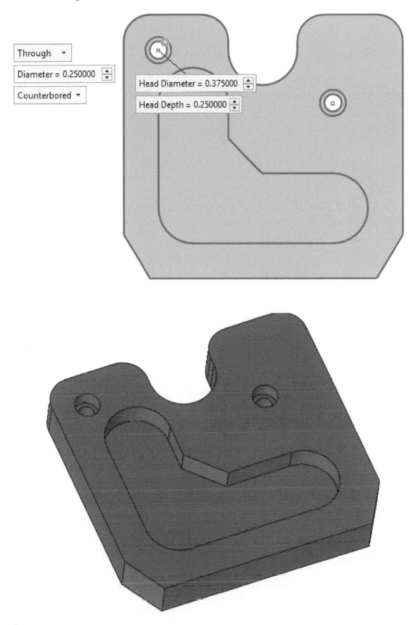

Save your work.

Design Exercise 6: 250

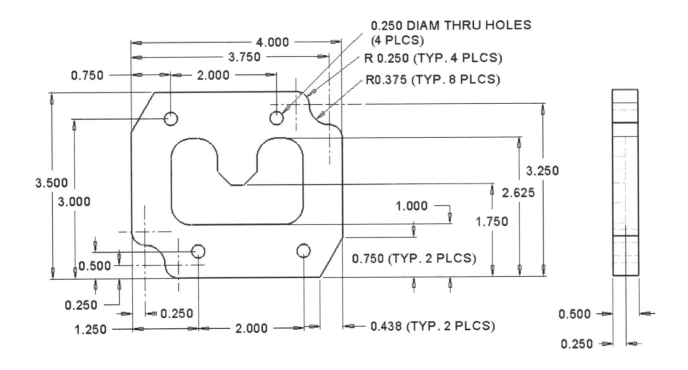

Sketch the main **4 x 3.5** rectangular shape, along with the **chamfers**. Anchor the sketch 1" from the UCS as shown.

Note: The 0.438 dimension only occurs once because the two chamfer lines were constructed parallel to each other. If this doesn't occur in your sketch, that's OK. Just dimension both of them fully.

Another note: Sometimes chamfers are designed into the sketch, while other times they're left out, only to create solid chamfer features after the sketch. This has to do with design intent, and how easy engineering changes can be made. If this were a really complicated sketch, it would be advisable to leave chamfers and radii out. In this case, however, we'll design them into the sketch.

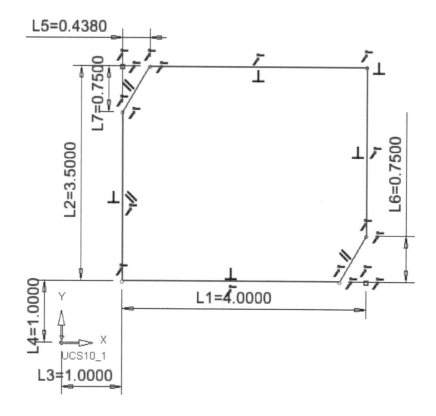

Exit the sketch and **extrude** it **0.500** deep.

Right-click on **extrude13** from the Feature Tree and select **Edit Reference Feature**. Sketch three circles in the upper right-hand corner and dimension them as shown below.

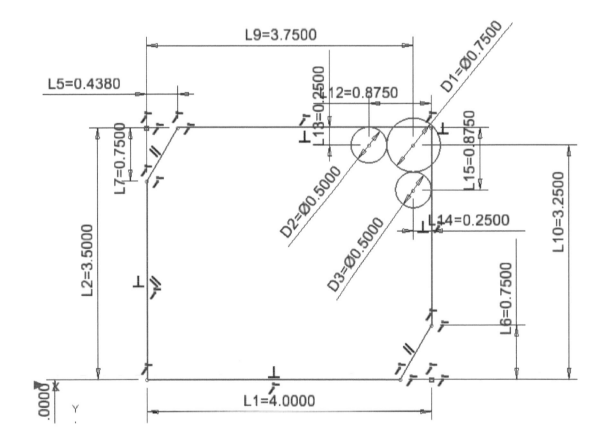

Trim the unwanted segments away.

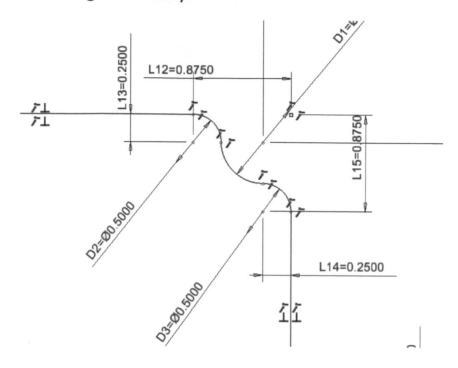

Exit the sketcher and watch as the model now includes the three corner radii.

Right-click on **extrude13** from the Feature Tree and select **Edit Reference Feature**. Sketch three circles in the lower left-hand corner and **dimension** them.

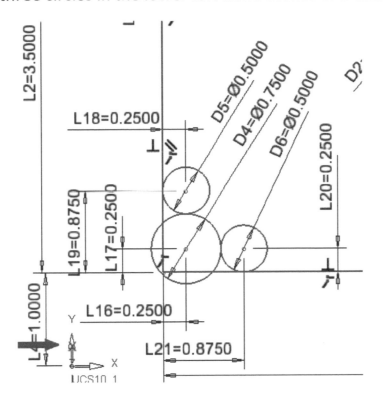

Trim the unwanted entities.

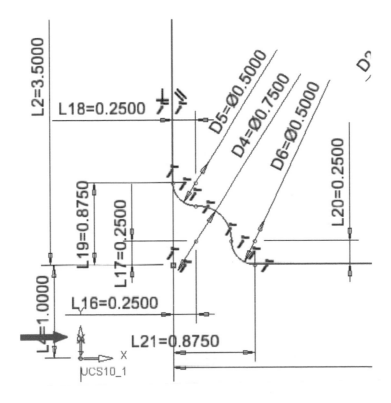

Press **OK** from the Feature Guide and observe the shape:

Sketch a rectangle on the top face and dimension. You'll need to add the left and bottom edges as **reference** lines to dimension from.

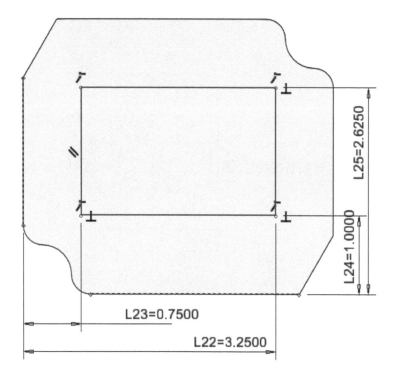

Sketch the notch and add dimensions:

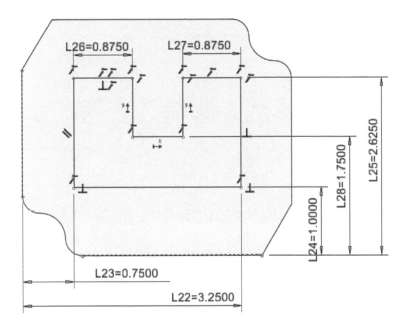

Exit the sketch and **extrude – remove** it **0.250** deep

Add two ¼" **chamfers** as solids features:

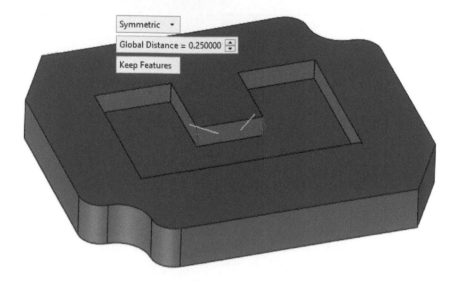

Add six 3/8" **rounds** as solids features:

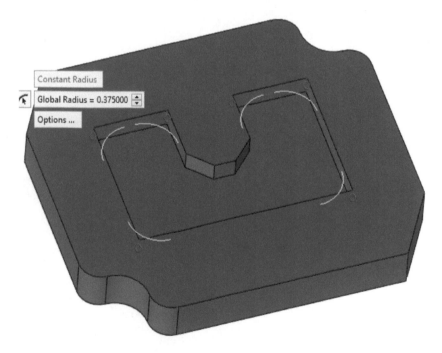

Sketch and dimension four circles on the top face to represent the four ¼"
through holes.

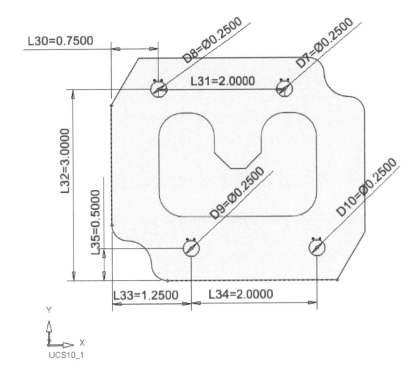

Exit the sketch and using **Solid > Extrude, Remove** the holes **through**.

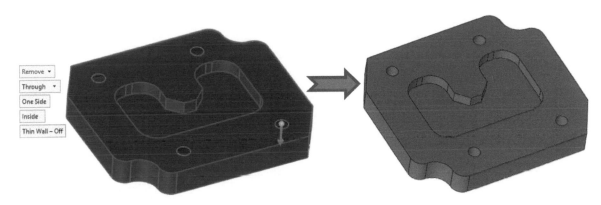

Save your work and submit your part file.

Chapter 7: Introduction to CAM

Overview

Cimatron has a powerful CAM package. It has the ability to program 2-5 axis toolpaths.

2-axis toolpaths include machining operations such as drilling, contouring, pocketing, and facing.

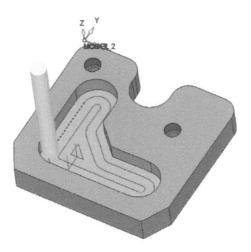

3-axis toolpaths include machining operations such as rough and re-rough machining, and a wide variety of surface finish machining.

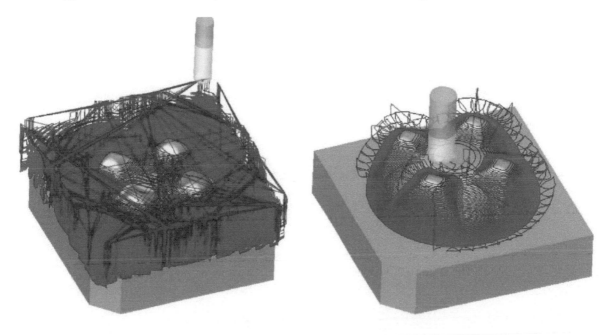

Rough Surface Machining   Finish Surface Machining

Since this course focuses on Cimatron basics, we'll concentrate on 2-axis toolpath machining. Once mastered, 3-axis machining is much easier. Because to learn how to program 2-axis toolpaths, you'll learn how to perform the following tasks—all of which are necessary to perform 3-axis machining.

- Define procedures (machining operation)
- Define the XY plane to orient machining
- Define cutting tools
- Define containment boundaries for contouring and pocketing
- Define feedrate and spindle speeds
- Learn how to navigate the toolpath programming panels

Remember from chapter 1 that parts are the core of Cimatron. Frpm parts we can create drawings, toolpaths, and more. But everything starts with a part. Therefore, to add toolpaths, we start with *referencing* an existing part.

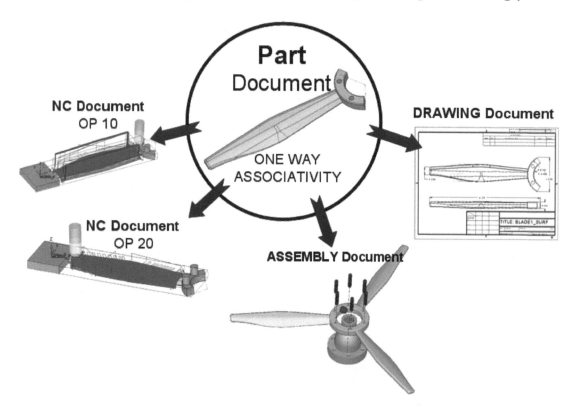

This allows for full associativity, meaning that when the part changes, so can the toolpaths, drawings, etc. This is a real time savings.

New NC Document

To program toolpaths, a new NC document must be created. This is accomplished by selecting File from the pulldown menus and selecting the NC_inch icon from the dialog.

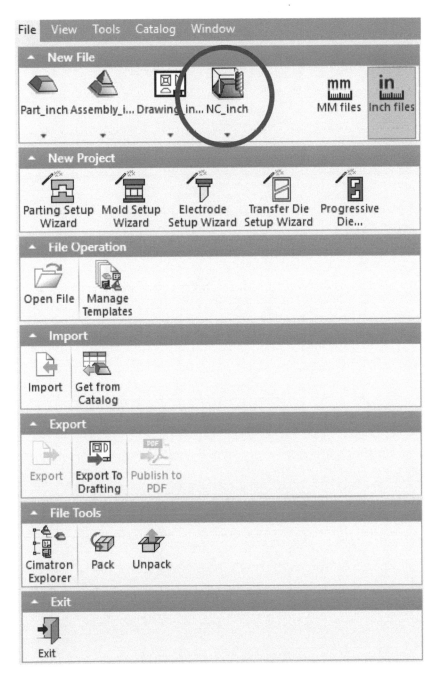

When selecting **NC Document**, the following wizard displays. It helps guide you through the CAM programming process.

Load Model

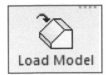

The first step is to load the desired CAD model to machine.

Upon selecting this icon, navigate and select a file you wish to load. Cimatron then loads the model and displays a menu.

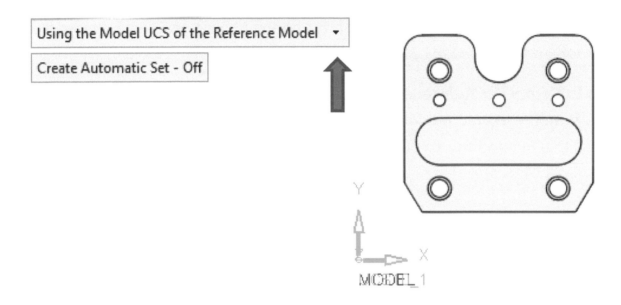

Select the arrowhead in the menu to display three options. If nothing is selected, the default selection is "**Using the Model UCS**".

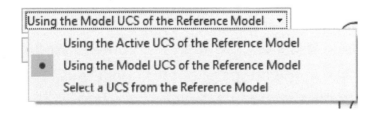

Using the Active UCS of the Reference Model: This relocates the loaded model such that the location and orientation of the active UCS will be moved to the location and orientation of MODEL UCS.

For example, let's say you created a UCS for the top of the part for machining named OP20, and one for the bottom of the part to be machined named OP10. And let's say you activated the OP10 UCS. In this case, the loaded model will be reoriented to the location and orientation of the MODEL UCS.

Using the Model UCS of the Reference Model: This positions the loaded model such that the location and orientation of the loaded MODEL UCS will be moved to the location and orientation of MODEL UCS.

Select a UCS from the Reference Model: This option allows you to choose from any UCS from the loaded model to be relocated to the location and orientation of the MODEL UCS. I find this to be the most useful when CAM programming.

NOTE: This step is critical. This defines the orientation of the part as it sets on the CNC machine. However you load this model, the machine tool operator must physically load the stock to machine the same way.

Remember parts are made in 3D space, and designers create them in whatever view is convenient to them. They generally don't anticipate how the part sits on a machine. And in many cases, we may have to orient the part more than one time to machine from different sides, e.g., top and bottom. This is our job as programmers. We decide how to position the part onto the machine.

If a mistake is made in this step, I strongly recommend starting over. It's possible to address the mistake in the program, but it's dangerous. CNC programmers are conservative and detailed oriented. Mistakes are not an option!

Once the above steps are completed, the following activities take place, not necessarily in any order:

- Cutting tools are defined
- Feedrate and spindle speeds are defined
- Toolpaths are created, along with all cutting paramaters
- Toolpath Simulation
- Post Processing

Simulation allows the programmer to visualize the toolpath before sending it to the shop floor. This is where we can catch mistakes, such as wrong orientation (step 3 above), too deep of cut, collisions, and much more.

Post Processing is the act of generating G & M code for the CNC machine. Post means *after*. Processing means to *generate*. Even in a small program, thousands of lines of G-code are generated in less than a second! Large programs for molds and dies can be millions of lines long.

Sample G-code program:

```
%
O272 (272 OP 30 )
G54 G90 G0 G40 G80 X-1.0 Y-1.0
( MILL OUTSIDE PROFILE - EXCLUDE LEFT CIRCLE)
T4 M6 (1/2 END MILL)
S4500 M3
G43 H4 Z.1 M8
G1 Z-.125 F10.0
G41 D5 X0 F18.0
Y3.423
X1.0 Y4.0
X6.0
Y0
X1.0
X-1.0
G40 Y-1.0
```

```
(PASS 2)
G1 Z-.25 F10.0
G41 D5 X0 F18.0
Y3.423
X1.0 Y4.0
X6.0
Y0
X1.0
X-1.0
G40 Y-1.0

G28 G91 G0 Z0
M30
%
```

NC Process Manager

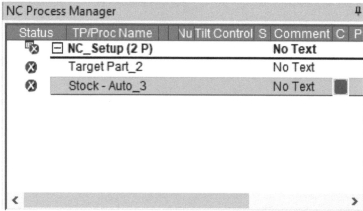

The **NC Process Manager** contains a sequential list of procedures in your program. Toolpaths can be reordered, edited, deleted, etc. I refer to it as a glorified setup sheet. It allows you to include comments to make it more friendly and readable.

Notice the red X's to the left of each procedure. That means their definitions are incomplete. Once complete, you'll see them replaced by green checkmarks.

Target Part: This is only used for toolpath *verification*. Different than simulation, this *compares* your toolpath(s) to the solid part model. It's useful for looking for areas you may have neglected. For example, the model may contain areas with a 1/16" radius at surface intersections, but the smallest corner radius you programmed for was 1/8".

We will not be using this feature at this level. Therefore, it can be deleted, or simply left alone. To delete it, right-click on the Target Part and select "Delete Procedure".

Stock – Auto: This allows you define the size and shape of the initial raw stock—before machining. In the beginning, it is not defined. It's listed in the NC Process Manager as a convenience so you don't forget to program it.

To define it, you can double-click on the procedure, or you can right-click and select Edit Procedure. It displays the following:

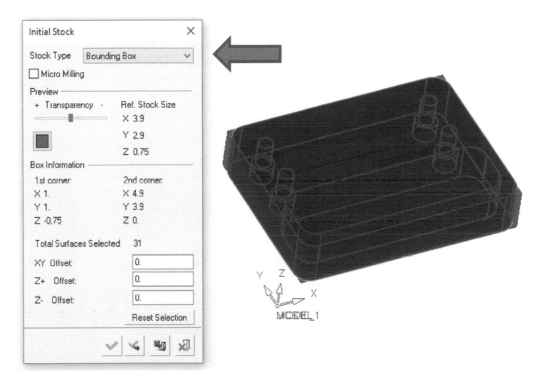

Stock Type: This defines the shape of the raw stock. The default shape is **Bounding Box**, allowing you to define a cubic shape, or billet stock. There are many other methods for defining the shape of the stock, but in this course we will stick to Bounding Box.

When selecting this procedure, it defaults to Bounding Box and preselects the entire solid model. The fields in the bottom allow you to add rough stock to the model, just as many billets of stock include.

The **green checkmark** allows to accept the parameters programmed and close the dialog. Now you should see a green checkmark next to the procedure in the NC Process Manager.

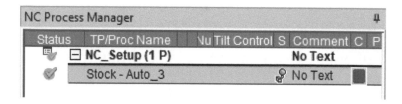

Toolpath

The next step is to define what Cimatron refers to as a *Toolpath*.

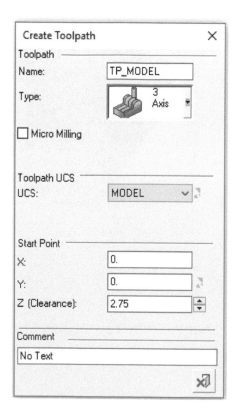

Type defines the type of programming, which includes 1-1/2, 3, 4, or 5-axis machining. I usually leave it set to **3-Axis**, which allows for 2-axis programming, as well as 3-axis surface machining. This is the most commonly purchased package.

Start Point allows you to define a starting position of the cutting tool, along with the default Z-clearance plane. I usually leave X and Y alone, but set the Z-axis to 0.100 for inch mode.

NOTE: Be sure to press the ENTER key when inputting numbers.

Comment allows you to include comments in your program. Your comment will be displayed in the NC Process Manager, and it will be included in the post processed G-code file for the machine tool operator to see. I strongly recommend programming comments so everyone knows what to expect in your program. For this toolpath, I would recommend including a comment such as OP10 or OP20.

Press the **green checkmark** upon completion of the toolpath definition.

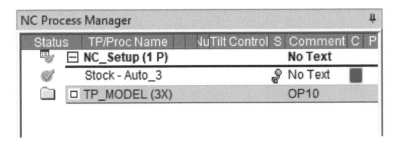

Procedure

Cimatron refers to all machining operations as ***procedures***. Remember from chapter 1 that Cimatron was developed in Israel and is used throughout the world. Therefore, *procedure* translates easier.

Procedures consist of drilling, contouring, pocketing, surface machining, and more.

Now that the model is loaded and properly oriented, the initial stock is defined, and the toolpath definition is complete, machining operations—or ***procedures***—can begin.

Procedures can be created two ways:

1. Right-click in the white (blank) area of the NC Process Manager. Then select New, followed by procedure.
2. Left-click the Procedure icon in the NC Wizard.

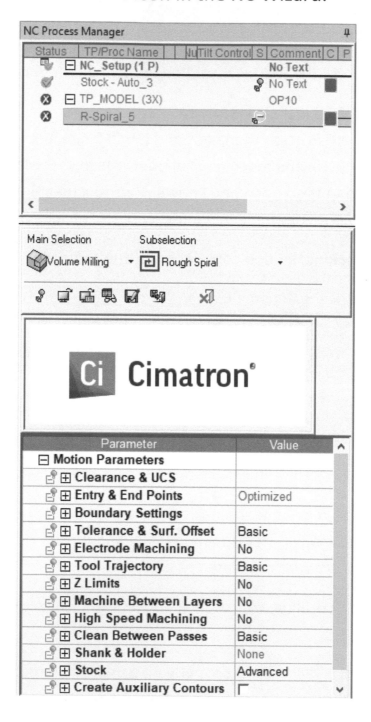

Next, take a closer look at the middle of this panel:

First, choose the *style* of milling from the **Main Selection**:

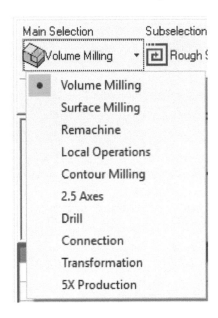

Then choose the *pattern* of milling from the **subselection**. This menu changes based on the style chosen from the Main Selection. In the example below, Volume Milling was chosen, and it offers these options of milling.

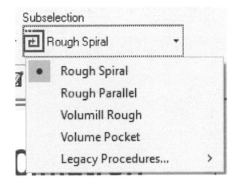

NOTE: Legacy Procedures refers to procedures from a long time ago. Just like many other CAM systems, Cimatron's procedures were updated to reflect the style of machining today. But to keep older customers who still use them, they kept the older style procedures. We will not explore these in this course.

When selecting 2.5 Axis from the Main Selection, the subselection offers the following:

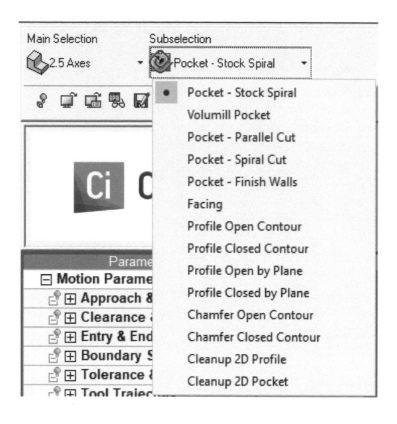

Pocket – Stock Spiral is the most common procedure chosen for removing inside pockets from models. Many programmers prefer a spiral motion that follows the boundary rather than parallel passes in the X or Y-axis.

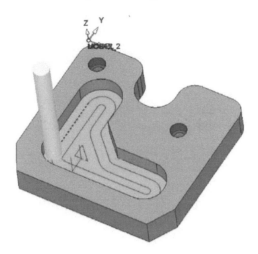

Facing is used to remove material from the top of the stock to produce a smoother finish and machine part thickness to size.

Profile is used to machine along one or more curves. The curves can be open or closed.

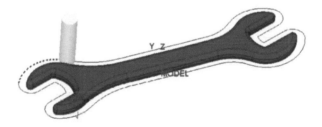

Chamfer is used to follow one or more curves to produce a chamfer with a chamfer cutting tool.

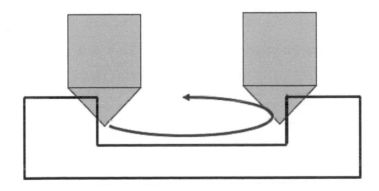

Procedure Parameters

Specific parameters change from procedure to procedure. However, many are the same. When Pocket – Stock Spiral is selected, the following parameters are displayed.

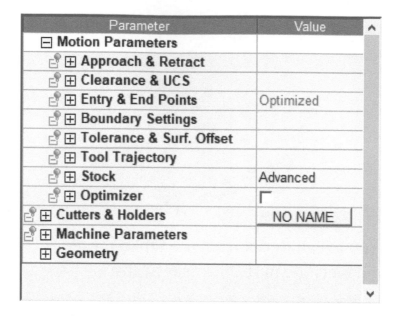

To minimize screen space, each heading is collapsed. To define parameters, click the + sign next to the heading you wish to change. Many of these parameters have default settings that work just fine. But I like to open (expand) each heading one by one to take a quick look.

At this point, I prefer is to define the contours to machine, followed by the tool definition. Many parameters default to a size relative to the tool diameter. If nothing is defined, the name of the tool is NO NAME and it's diameter is 0.3937.

So I generally select Cutters & Holders first from this dialog and define a cutting tool. Refer to Cutters and Holders in the next section for details.

Next, I prefer to define the contour to cut along. This is accomplished by expanding the Geometry options and selecting from the dialog.

Geometry	
Part Contours	0
Stock Contours	0

Part Contours allows me to define the shape to machine. The 0 in the field to the right tells me that no contours have been selected yet. Therefore, click on the 0 to display the contour dialog.

Advanced Selection allows you to define the contour to machine. You'll be prompted to pick the first and last curve to machine. They'll be chained together. Press the green checkmark to identify completion of the contour.

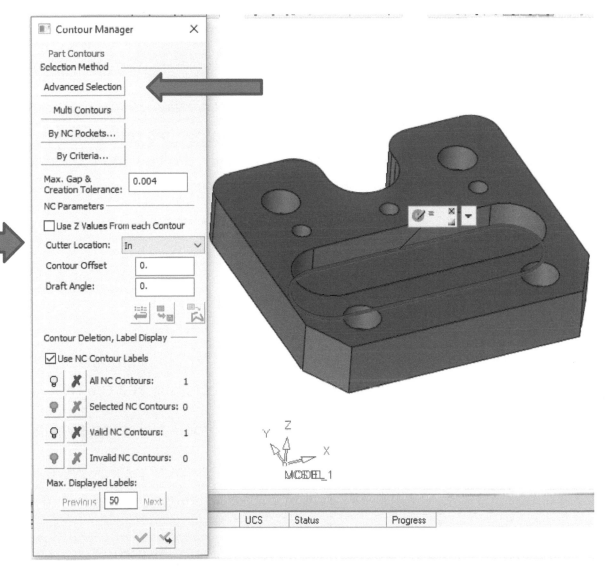

IMPORTANT: The next thing to look at is the Cutter Location. Because this was a pocket, Cimatron was smart enough to guess you want the tool on the inside. But when contouring (profiling), it doesn't know. Therefore, be sure to watch this field.

Optionally, you can define an offset from the contour. This is useful when you want to rough machine and leave stock for finish machining.

Press the green checkmark when the contour definition and parameters are complete.

Approach and Retract:

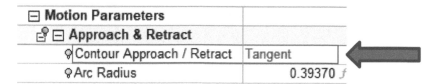

This controls how the cutting tool approaches the contour and retracts away. The default setting is **Normal**, which means the cutter feeds directly into the work piece, producing a small blemish upon entry.

The preferred method is **Tangent**:

A tangential entry and retract causes the tool to "*arc*" into the contour, resulting in a less impactful entry. This is the preferred method of entry and retract.

Notice the **Arc radius** is predefined to 0.3937. It's automatically set to a value equal to the tool diameter. Normally this is fine, so I don't change it.

Clearance & UCS:

The next heading to look at is the Clearance Planes.

⊟ Clearance & UCS	
♀Use Clearance	☑
♀Clearance Plane	0.10000 *f*
♀Internal Clearance	Absolute Z
♀Absolute Z	0.10000 *f*
♀UCS Name	MODEL
♀Create UCS	Access
♀Machine Preview	Access

The clearance plane is the Z-axis value the tool will rapid traverse to before machining. In inch mode, it's common to set the clearance planes to 0.1 inches. This default value was defined during the toolpath definition. So I generally don't change anything here.

Entry & End Points:

The next heading to look at is the Entry & End Points.

⊟ Entry & End Points	Optimized
♀Ramp Angle	90.00000 *f*
♀Min. Plunge Size	0.00000 *f*
♀DZ/Feed Start	0.03937 *f*

Ramp Angle defines the angle at which the tool approaches the first cut. In the case of a 2D contour (profile), 90 degrees is fine. But when pocketing, it's not recommended to let the tool plunge directly into the stock at entry. It's preferred to helically enter, like that of a cork screw. When entering steel, you may want to change the angle from 90 degrees to 1 to 3. When cutting aluminum, you may prefer 10 degrees.

Minimum Plunge Size defines the smallest area you wish for the cutter to engage. The value entered plus the cutter diameter is the smallest area the cutter can plunge into. I usually leave this setting alone.

DZ/Feed Start is the Z-axis value the tool starts machining from. DZ stands for Delta Z. I don't really like using a Delta Z from the clearance plane, so I always set this equal to my clear plane, or 0.100 in this case.

Boundary Settings:

This heading allows you to modify the boundary—in case you didn't set these during contour definition.

Boundary Settings		
♀Cutter Location (common)	In	
♀Contour Offset (common)		0.00000 ƒ
♀Draft Angle (common)		0.00000

Tolerance and Surf. Offset:

This heading allows you to define machining tolerances. The default Contour tolerance is 0.00039 because it's a metric based system. I generally change this to 0.001 or 0.0001, based upon the what I'm trying to achieve. For 2D procedures, 0.001 is accurate enough. For rough surface machining, I may use 0.010. And for finish surface machining I may choose something as tight as 0.0001

Tolerance & Surf. Offset	
♀Contour Offset (Rough)	0.00000 ƒ
♀Entry Offset	0.27500 ƒ
♀Contour Tolerance	0.00039 ƒ
♀Max. Contour Gap	0.00400

Tool Trajectory:

This heading allows you to define the top of the part, the depth at which to machine, max depth of cut (down step), how many down steps, side stepover amount, and cutting mode (Climb or Conventional).

Tool Trajectory	
Z Values source	General Values
Z-Top	0.06063 *f*
Z-Bottom	-0.18937 *f*
Down Step	0.25000 *f*
Mill Finish Pass	☐
Side Step	0.30000 *f*
Corner Milling	External Round
Cutting Mode	Climb
Collapsing	Region

Stock:

This heading allows you to update the stock after every each procedure. The default condition is YES.

Stock	Advanced
Update Remaining Stock	Yes

Cutters and Holders

Cutters—or Cutting tools—can be defined on the fly (as needed) or called from a library. We will define them as needed in our exercises.

Cutting tools come in three basics shapes:

1. Flat: flat on the ends with sharp corners
2. Ball Nose: Full radius on the end of the cutting tool
3. Bull Nose: Flat end mill with corner radii

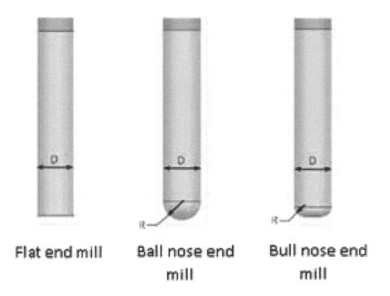

Flat end mill   Ball nose end mill   Bull nose end mill

Holders are the mechanism that *holds*—or secures—cutting tools. There are a variety of types, all outside the scope of this course.

ER32 Cutting Tool Holder

Tools are assigned to a magazine pockets in the CNC machine. Machines hold from 10 to hundreds of cutting tools. Tools are called up from a CNC programs as needed. The following sample code performs a **Tool Change**.

T1 M6

T1 rotates tool magazine position 1 into the *ready* position.

M6 instructs the tool change arm to take the tool from the magazine and place it into the spindle. What's the in the spindle gets returned to the magazine. Some machines take seconds to perform this operation. High speed machines perform this operation in less than a second.

Cutting Tool Parameters:

In general you'll program the following parameters each time you need a new cutting tool:

- Tool Number (magazine number)
- Tool type (Flat, Ball, or Bull)
- Tool Diameter
- Flute length (maximum depth of cut)
- Length of tool (length from tip of tool to the holder)

Additional parameters can be programmed for the **holder**. This is used to prevent collisions—especially when 5-axis programming. At this level, holders are not a concern, so we won't program them.

To define a new cutting tool, select the Cutters icon from the wizard on the left.

This displays the tools page. This example shows 6 inputs.

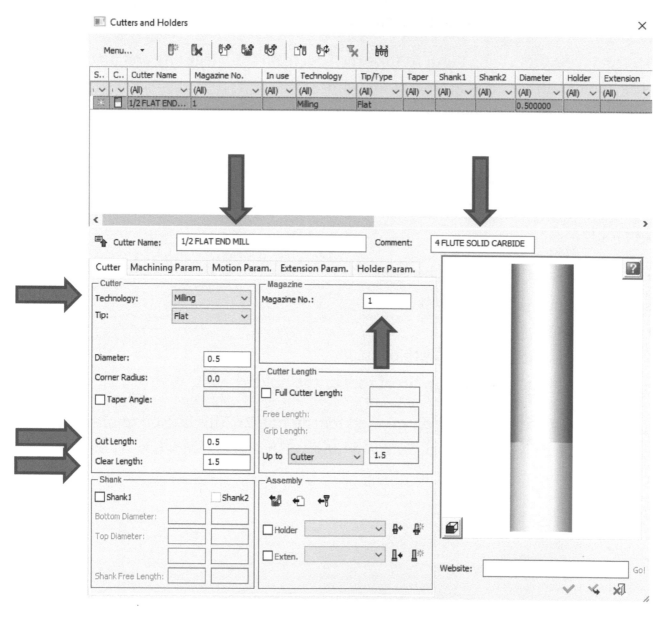

Upon completion of the cutting tool, press the **_large green checkmark_** in the lower right-hand corner. Should you choose to create more tools, select **_Apply_** instead.

Chapter 8: 2D CAM Exercises

2D CAM Exercise 1: Cardholder Base

This exercise guides you through the following:

- UCS definition (OP20)
- Setup
- 2D Profile
- 2D Pocket

Create UCS Definition (OP20):

Open the previously created model named **Cardholder**.

Select the UCS Manager from the top:

Turn off the **UCS10_1** by toggling the lightbulb. Then press OK (green checkmark).

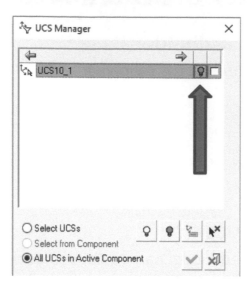

Select the arrowhead from the UCS Definition icon at the top:

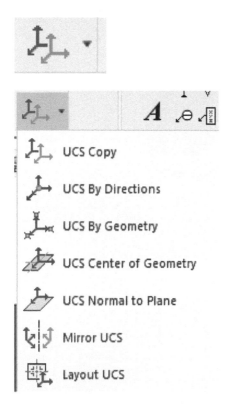

Select **UCS Center of Geometry**, drag a window around the part, and press your middle mouse (exit).

Make the following changes:

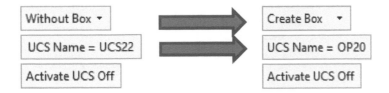

Cimatron offers a grid of points on each side, top, and bottom. Rotate the model until you can see the small point at top-dead center. Pick this point to locate the UCS and select the green checkmark.

Select **Save** from the File menu and save it (same name).

Select **Close** from the File menu.

Select File > New File > **NC_inch**

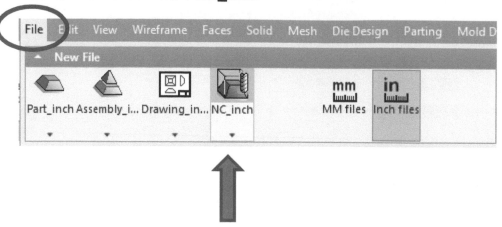

Select the **Load Model** icon from the NC Wizard.

Navigate accordingly and choose the **Cardholder** from the File Navigator.

Cimatron needs to know where to place this model, and how to orient it for machining. Choose "**Select a UCS from the Reference Model**".

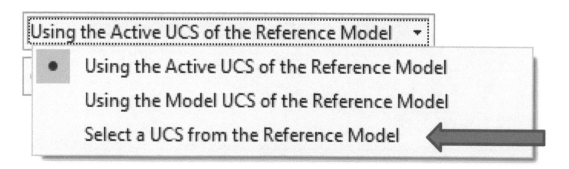

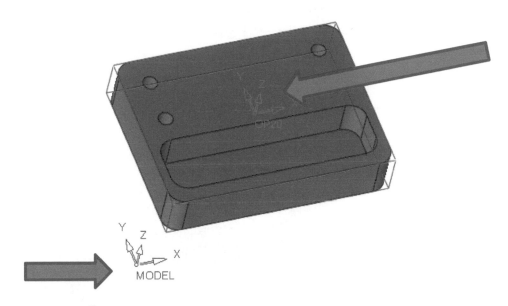

Pick the **OP20** UCS from the top-center of the model. The model will move as soon as you make the pick. Now both UCS's are in the same location. Then select OK (green checkmark) from the Feature Guide to complete the operation.

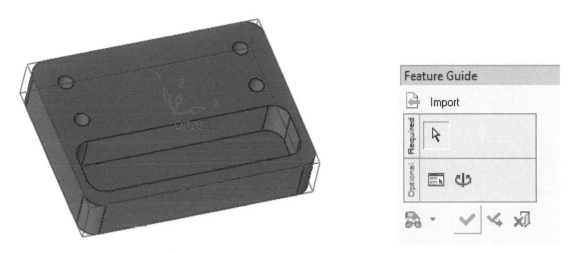

Note: If you don't see the green checkmark, move your cursor into the general area so it pops up. There could be a graphics card issue.

STOCK:

Double-click the **Stock - Auto** procedure and press **OK** (green checkmark). This creates the initial stock the exact size of the part.

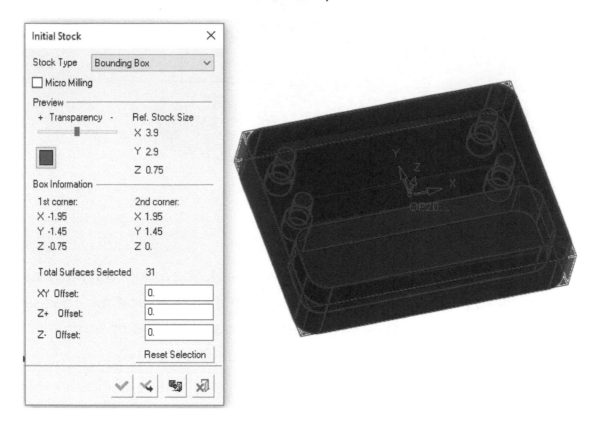

PART:

Right-click on **Target Pa**rt from the NC Process Manager, then select **Delete Procedure** from the submenu.

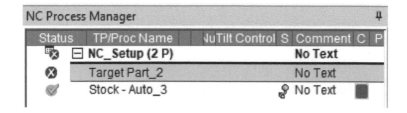

TOOLPATH:

The next step is to create a **Toolpath**. This defines the type of machining (2-5 axis), the UCS to use (MODEL), start point, clearance plane, and allows for a comment.

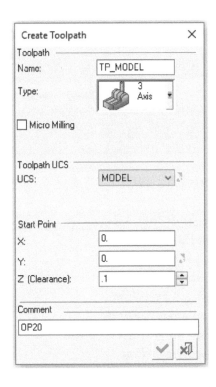

We'll stick with 3-axis machining, because this allows for 2D machining, as well. Change the Z Clearance Plane to 0.1 And insert a comment to read "OP20". Then press OK.

Notice the update to the NC Process Manager:

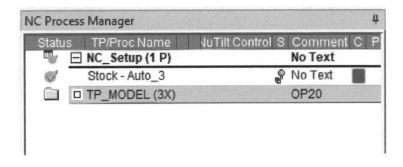

PROCEDURE

Select the Procedure icon from the NC wizard. Optionally, you can right click in the white space of the NC Process Manager and choose Create Procedure.

Set the **Main Selection to 2.5 Axes**. Set the **Subselection to Profile Closed Contour**.

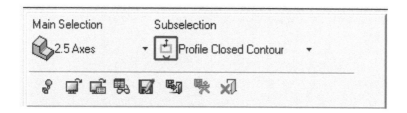

The following parameters must be set.

Parameter	Value
⊟ **Motion Parameters**	
⊞ **Approach & Retract**	
⊞ **Clearance & UCS**	
⊞ **Entry & End Points**	Optimized
⊞ **Boundary Settings**	
⊞ **Tolerance & Surf. Offset**	
⊞ **Tool Trajectory**	
⊞ **Stock**	Advanced
⊞ **Optimizer**	☐
⊞ **Cutters & Holders**	NO NAME
⊞ **Machine Parameters**	
⊞ **Geometry**	

As indicated in the overview, I like to create a tool first, then define the profile geometry to cut.

Select NO NAME from **Cutters & Holders**. NO NAME is the default cutter, so let's define a new one.

Select the **NEW CUTTER** icon from the very top – near the left.

- Set the Cutter Name to: ½" END MILL
- Change the comment to: 4 FLUTE SOLID CARBIDE
- Change the Magazine Number to: 1
                                                          Answer YES to the prompt
- Change the Diameter to: 0.5
- Change Cut Length to: 0.5
- Change Clear Length to: 1.25

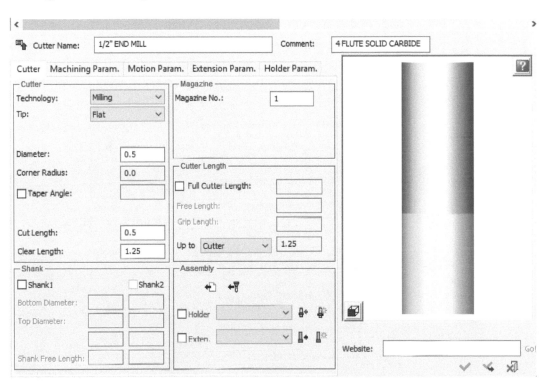

Press **OK**.

Click the **plus sign** to the left of **Geometry** to expand the options.

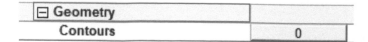

⊟ Geometry	
Contours	0

Click the 0 to display the Control Manager. This allows you to define the geometry to cut, along with some parameters.

Change the Milling Side from Inside to **Outside**.

Select **Advanced Selection** (near the top).

Change Chain to **Faces Outer Boundary**. Then pick the top face of the model.

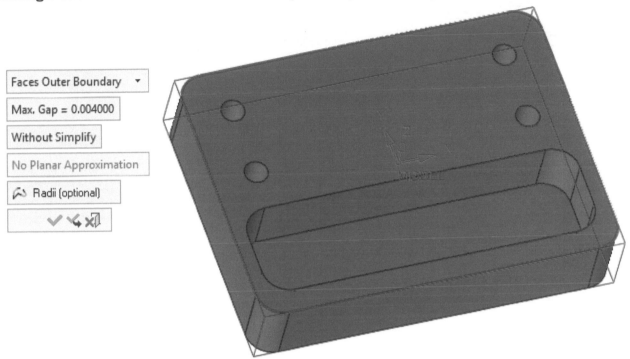

Press **OK** (green checkmark).

Press **OK** from the Control Manager dialog to complete the definition.

⊞ Cutters & Holders	1/2 END MILL
⊞ Machine Parameters	
⊟ Geometry	
Contours	1

Approach & Retract: Press the plus sign to expand the options. Change both Normals to **Tangent**. Press the minus sign to collapse the list.

Entry & End Points: Change DZ Feed/Start from 0.03937 to 0.100

Tolerance & Surf. Offset: Change the **Contour Tolerance** to 0.001

Tool Trajectory: Set the parameters as shown below:

Tool Trajectory	
Z Values source	General Values
Z-Top	0.00000 f
Z-Bottom	-0.75000 f
Down Step	0.75000 f
Stock Width	0.00000 f
Trim Loops	Global
Spline Approximation	Linear
Cutting Technique	Standard
Corner Milling	Sharp Corner
Cutting Mode	Climb

Machine Parameters: Change spindle speed (Spin) to 5000. Change Feed to 50. Change Coolant to Flood.

Machine Parameters	
Feed and Spin Calculator	Access
Vc (feet/min)	654.49847
Spin	5000
Feed (inch/min)	50.00000
Air Motions	Rapid
Plunge Feed (%)	30
Corner Feed (%)	75
Enable Cutter Compensation	No
Coolant	Flood
Spindle Direction	Clockwise
Rotary Axis Preferred Positio	None

Save & Calculate:

As this completes the settings, press the icon shown below to **Save & Calculate** the procedure.

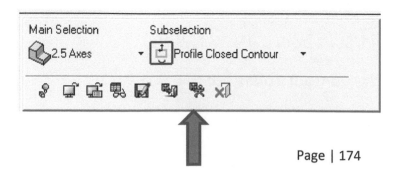

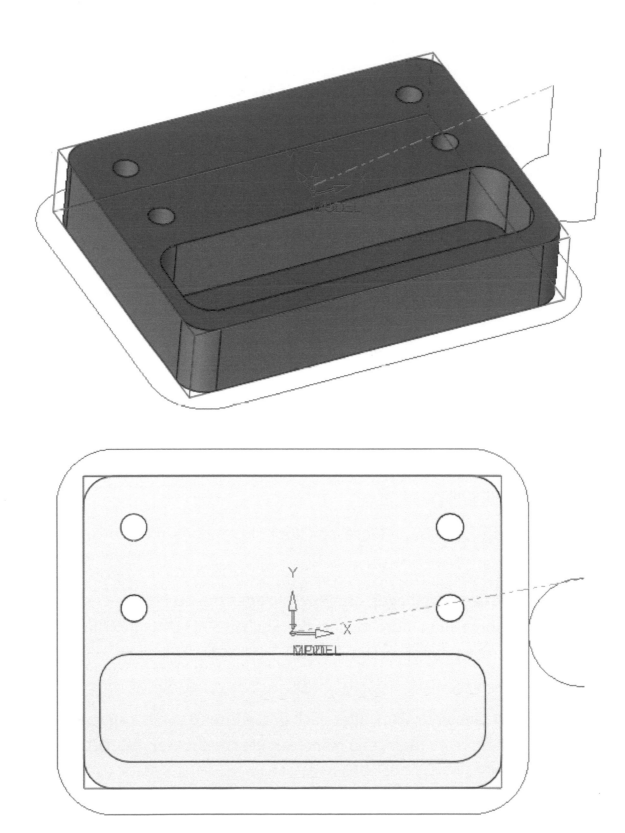

Select the **Navigator** icon and press the Movie Forward button to view the cutter path in wireframe mode. Notice the direction is—in general—clockwise. This represents Climb milling. Notice the depth of cut is at the bottom of the part. And notice the tangent move as it enter the work piece and tangent move as it exits.

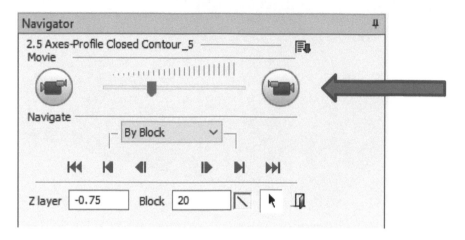

You can also view the cutter path Block by Block. A Block is a line of code. By clicking the arrows forward and back you can view the path. This is convenient when searching for collisions, etc.

To exit the Navigator, press the **Close** icon (looks like a door in the lower right-hand corner).

Observe the **NC Process Manager**, as it now includes the 2D Profile. Click **No Text** and change it to something more meaningful, such as **Prof Outside**. This will be helpful in the future as the programs grows.

Save As Main

It's a good idea to save your work after each procedure to avoid losing any of your work. Select File > Save As Main, and name this file **Cardholder_NC_OP20**.

POCKET:

Click the **Procedure** icon from the NC Wizard and change the Subselection menu to **Pocket – Stock Spiral**.

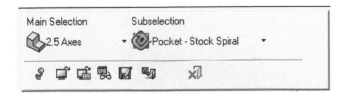

Many of the parameters remain the same from the previous procedure, some need to change, while others can remain.

The following parameters can remain the same:
- Approach & Retract
- Clearance & UCS
- Cutters & Holders
- Machine Parameters (Feed & Spindle speed)

Geometry: Expand the Geometry menus and observe that 1 part contour is defined. This is leftover from the last procedure and won't work for the pocket. Therefore, click on the 1, then right-click in the graphics screen and select **Reset All**, followed by **YES** to the prompt.

The cutter location is preset to cut on the inside, so no changes are necessary here.

Press **Advanced Selection**, change Chain to **Faces Outer Boundary**, then pick the floor (face) at the bottom of the pocket.

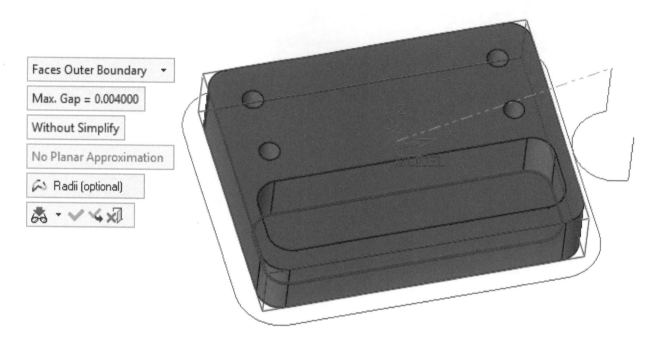

Press **OK**. Then press **OK** from the **Contour Manager**.

Tool Trajectory:

Change Z-Bottom to -0.625 and Down Sep to 0.650

Tool Trajectory	
Z Values source	General Values
Z-Top	0.00000 f
Z-Bottom	-0.65000 f
Down Step	0.65000 f
Mill Finish Pass	☐
Side Step	0.30000 f
Corner Milling	External Round
Cutting Mode	Climb
Collapsing	Region

Save & Calculate the procedure and observe the cutter path.

Use the **Navigator** to watch the pocketing operation.

NOTE: This may not be the most preferred method of pocketing, but at this level it taught you how to perform the procedure. Later on we'll learn how to modify procedures. Then we might consider a smaller tool, a ramp angle, etc.

Select File and **Save**.

2D CAM Exercise 2: Mill301

This exercise guides you through the following:

- UCS definition (OP20)
- Setup
- 2D Profile
- 2D Pocket
- Drill & Counterbore

Create UCS Definition (OP10):

Open the previously created model named *Mill301*.

Select the **UCS Manager** from the top:

Turn off the **UCS10_1** by toggling the lightbulb. Then press **OK** (green checkmark).

Select the arrowhead from the UCS Definition icon at the top:

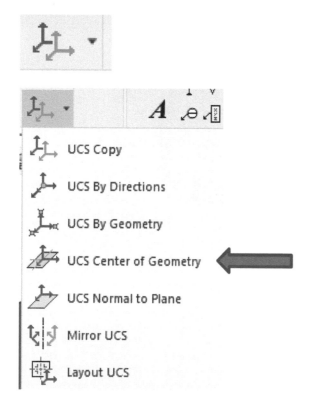

Select **UCS Center of Geometry**, drag a window around the part, and press your middle mouse (exit).

Make the following changes:

Cimatron offers a grid of points to choose from on each side, top, and bottom. Rotate the model until you can see the small point at top-dead center. Pick this point to locate the UCS and select the green checkmark.

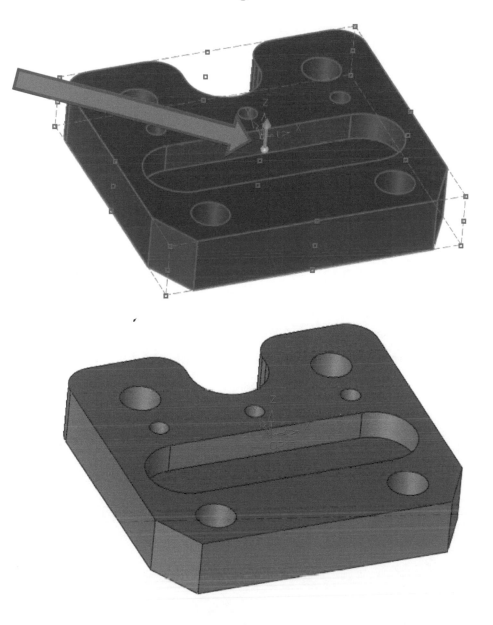

Select **Save** from the File menu and save it (same name).

Select **Close** from the File menu.

Select File > New File > **NC_inch**

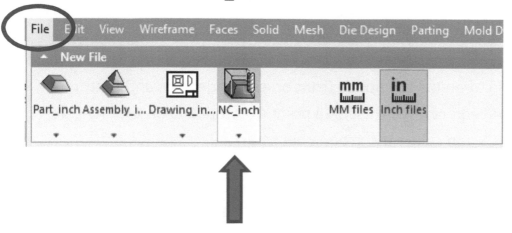

Select the **Load Model** icon from the NC Wizard.

Navigate accordingly and choose the **Mill301** from the File Navigator.

Cimatron needs to know where to place this model, and how to orient it for machining. Choose "**Select a UCS from the Reference Model**".

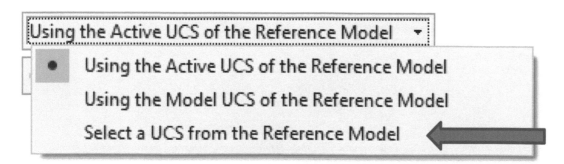

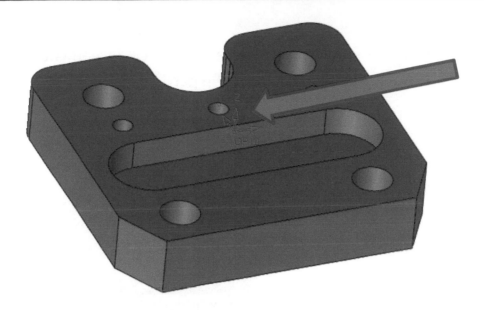

Pick the **OP10** UCS from the top-center of the model. The model will move as soon as you make the pick. Now both UCS's are in the same location. Then select **OK** (green checkmark) from the Feature Guide to complete the operation.

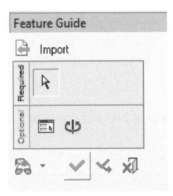

Note: If you don't see the green checkmark, move your cursor into the general area so it pops up. There could be a graphics card issue.

STOCK:

Double-click the **Stock - Auto** procedure and press **OK** (green checkmark). This creates the initial stock the exact size of the part.

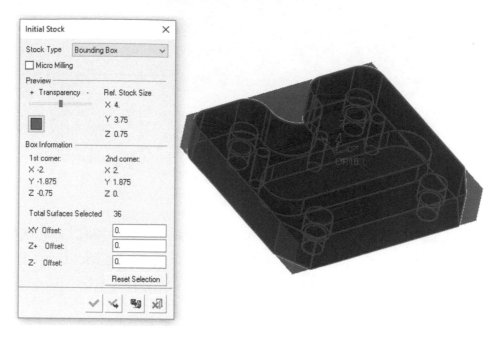

PART:

Right-click on **Target Part** from the NC Process Manager, then select **Delete Procedure** from the submenu.

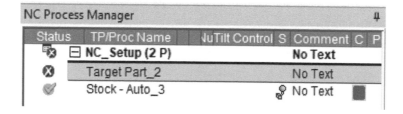

TOOLPATH:

The next step is to create a **Toolpath**. This defines the type of machining (2-5 axis), the UCS to use (MODEL), start point, clearance plane, and allows for a comment.

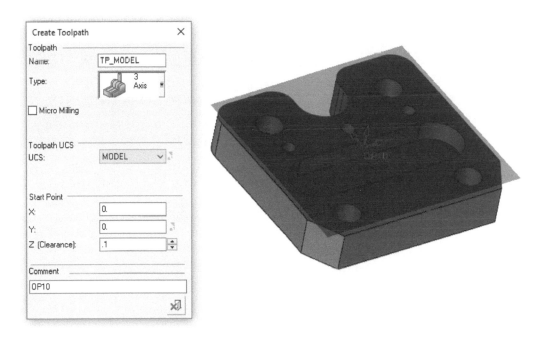

Set your Clearance Plane to 0.1 and observe the graphic representation above the part. This is the only time you'll ever see this clear plane, so be sure it's set correctly.

We'll stick with 3-axis machining, because this allows for 2D machining, as well. Insert a comment to read "**OP10**". Then press **OK**.

Notice the update to the NC Process Manager:

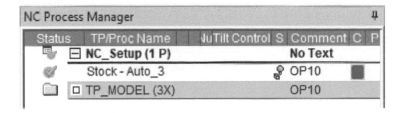

PROCEDURE

Select the Procedure icon from the NC wizard. Optionally, you can right click in the white space of the NC Process Manager and choose Create Procedure.

Set the **Main Selection to 2.5 Axes**. Set the **Subselection to Profile Closed Contour**.

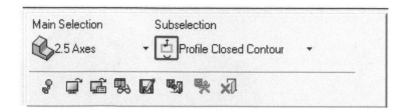

The following parameters must be set.

Parameter	Value
⊟ **Motion Parameters**	
⊞ **Approach & Retract**	
⊞ **Clearance & UCS**	
⊞ **Entry & End Points**	Optimized
⊞ **Boundary Settings**	
⊞ **Tolerance & Surf. Offset**	
⊞ **Tool Trajectory**	
⊞ **Stock**	Advanced
⊞ **Optimizer**	⌐
⊞ **Cutters & Holders**	NO NAME
⊞ **Machine Parameters**	
⊞ **Geometry**	

As indicated in the overview, I like to create a tool first, then define the profile geometry to cut. This is because Cimatron uses variables for default values. For example, the value of the tangent approach is set to the diameter of the tool. Therefore, when you define the tool diameter first, many of the default conditions are fine.

Select **NO NAME** from **Cutters & Holders**. NO NAME is the default cutter, so let's define a new one.

Select the **NEW CUTTER** icon from the very top – near the left.

- Set the Cutter Name to: **½" END MILL**
- Change the comment to: **4 FLUTE SOLID CARBIDE**
- Change the Magazine Number to: **1**
                                                        Answer YES to the prompt
- Change the Diameter to: **0.5**
- Change Cut Length to: **0.5**
- Change Clear Length to: **1.25**

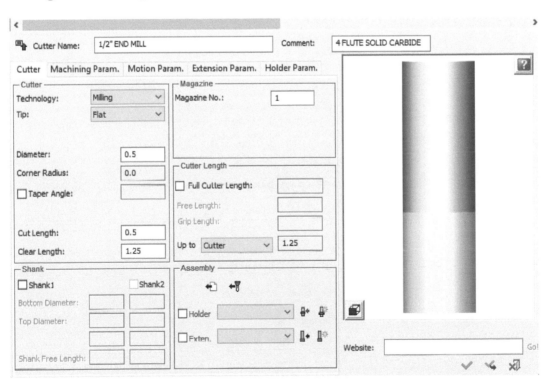

Press **OK**.

The next thing I like to do is define the geometry to machine. Click the **plus sign** to the left of **Geometry** to expand the options.

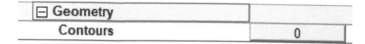

⊟ Geometry	
Contours	0

Click the 0 to display the Control Manager. This allows you to define the geometry to cut, along with some parameters.

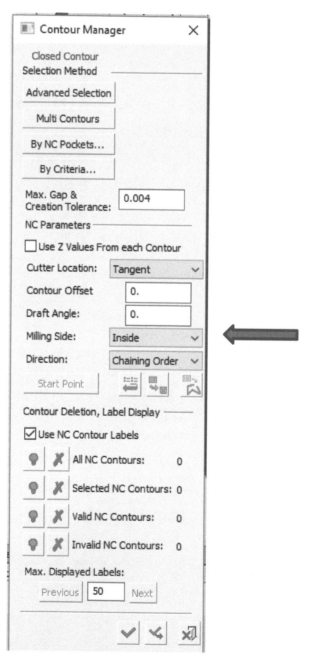

Change the Milling Side from Inside to **Outside**.

Select **Advanced Selection** (near the top).

Change Chain to **Faces Outer Boundary**. Then pick the top face of the model.

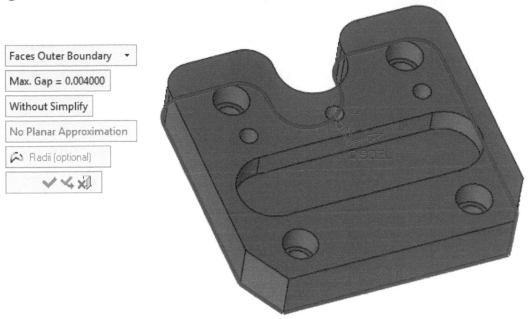

Press **OK** (green checkmark).

Press **OK** from the Control Manager dialog to complete the definition.

⊞ Cutters & Holders	1/2 END MILL
⊞ Machine Parameters	
⊟ Geometry	
Contours	1

Approach & Retract: Press the plus sign to expand the options. Change both Normals to **Tangent**. Press the minus sign to collapse the list.

Entry & End Points: Change DZ Feed/Start from 0.03937 to **0.100**

Tolerance & Surf. Offset: Change the **Contour Tolerance** to **0.001**

Tool Trajectory: Set the parameters as shown below:

Tool Trajectory	
Z Values source	General Values
Z-Top	0.00000 _f_
Z-Bottom	-0.75000 _f_
Down Step	0.75000 _f_
Stock Width	0.00000 _f_
Trim Loops	Global
Spline Approximation	Linear
Cutting Technique	Standard
Corner Milling	Sharp Corner
Cutting Mode	Climb

Machine Parameters: Change spindle speed (Spin) to **5000**. Change Feed to **50**. Change Coolant to **Flood**.

Machine Parameters	
Feed and Spin Calculator	Access
Vc (feet/min)	654.49847
Spin	5000
Feed (inch/min)	50.00000
Air Motions	Rapid
Plunge Feed (%)	30
Corner Feed (%)	75
Enable Cutter Compensation	No
Coolant	Flood
Spindle Direction	Clockwise
Rotary Axis Preferred Positio	None

Save & Calculate:

As this completes the settings, press the icon shown below to **Save & Calculate** the procedure.

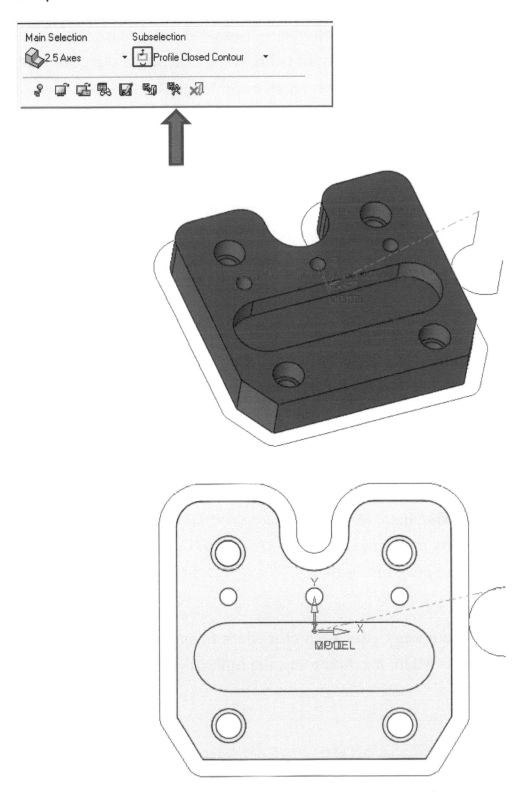

Select the **Navigator** icon and press the Movie Forward button to view the cutter path in wireframe mode. Notice the direction is—in general—clockwise. This represents Climb milling. Notice the depth of cut is at the bottom of the part. And notice the tangent move as it enter the work piece and tangent move as it exits.

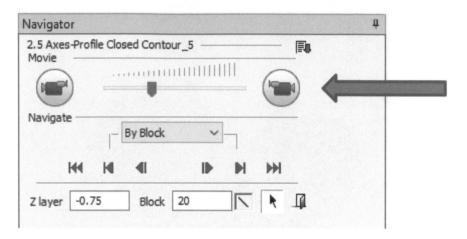

You can also view the cutter path Block by Block. A Block is a line of code. By clicking the arrows forward and back you can view the path. This is convenient when searching for collisions, etc.

To exit the Navigator, press the **Close** icon (looks like a door in the lower right-hand corner).

Observe the **NC Process Manager**, as it now includes the 2D Profile. Click **No Text** and change it to something more meaningful, such as **Prof Outside**. This will be helpful in the future as the programs grows.

Save As Main

It's a good idea to save your work after each procedure to avoid losing any of your work. Select **File > Save As Main**, and name this file **Mill301_NC_OP10**.

POCKET:

Click the **Procedure** icon from the NC Wizard and change the Subselection menu to **Pocket – Stock Spiral**.

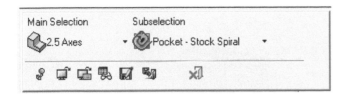

Many of the parameters remain the same from the previous procedure, some need to change, while others can remain.

The following parameters can remain the same:
- Approach & Retract
- Clearance & UCS
- Cutters & Holders
- Machine Parameters (Feed & Spindle speed)

Geometry: Expand the Geometry menus and observe that 1 part contour is defined. This is leftover from the last procedure and won't work for the pocket. Therefore, click on the 1, then right-click in the graphics screen and select **Reset All**, followed by **YES** to the prompt.

The cutter location is preset to cut on the inside, so no changes are necessary here.

Press **Advanced Selection**, change Chain to **Faces Outer Boundary**, then pick the floor (face) at the bottom of the pocket.

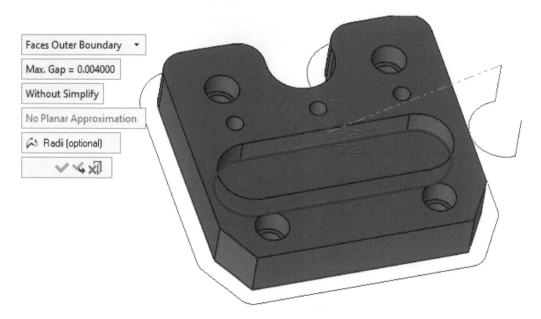

Press **OK**. Then press **OK** from the **Contour Manager**.

Tool Trajectory:

Change Z-Bottom to -0.375 and Down Sep to 0.370

Tool Trajectory	
Z Values source	General Values
Z-Top	0.00000 f
Z-Bottom	-0.37500 f
Down Step	0.37500 f
Mill Finish Pass	☐
Side Step	0.30000 f
Corner Milling	External Round
Cutting Mode	Climb
Collapsing	Region

Save & Calculate the procedure and observe the cutter path.

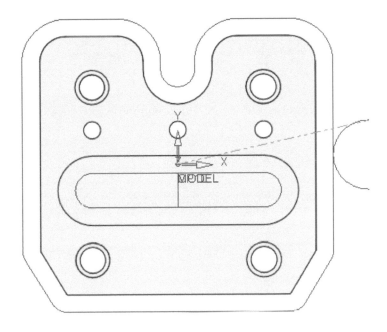

Use the **Navigator** to watch the pocketing operation.

NOTE: This may not be the most preferred method of pocketing, so this time let's use a smaller tool.

Edit the Pocket:

There are two ways to edit procedures. You may choose either of the following:

1. Right-click on **2X-Pocket** in the NC Process Manager. Then select **Edit > Edit Procedure Parameters**.

   --or—

2. **Double click** on the procedure **2X-Pocket**

Either option brings the original parameters back up for you to make changes.

Left-click on the ½" **END MILL** to the right of Cutters & Holders so you can define a smaller diameter cutter.

Select the **New Tool** icon from the top.

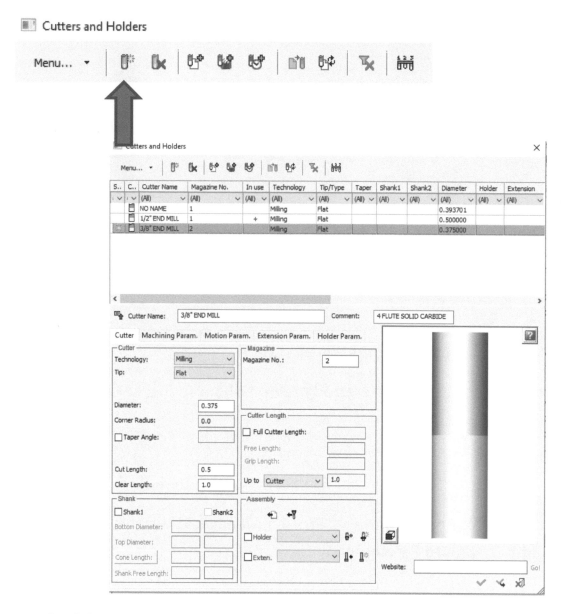

Set the following parameters as shown above:

- Cutter Name: **3/8" END MILL**
- Comment: **4 FLUTE SOLID CARBIDE**
- Magazine No: **2**
- Cut Length: **0.5**
- Clear Length: **1.0**

Click **OK** to exit the Cutters & Holders Manager.

Save & Calculate the procedure and observe the cutter path:

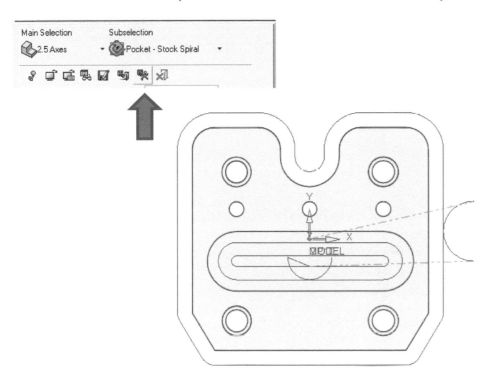

This cutterpath is better because the 3/8" end mill has more room to cut than the crowded ½" end mill. Rotate to an isometric orientation and use the Navigator to observe the path.

But notice the tool plunges straight down into the workpiece to full depth before machining along X and Y. Plunging into steel at 90 degrees is strongly discouraged because it's likely to break the tool. Ramping the tool into the workpiece at a small angle works better. 1 to 3 degrees for steel works fine. 10 degrees for aluminum works fine. It may be fine to plunge at 90 degrees into wax, wood, and graphite.

Edit the **2X-Pocket** once again.

Expand **Entry & End Points** and change the **Ramp Angle** from 90 to to **3** degrees.

Entry & End Points	Optimized
Ramp Angle	3.00000 *f*
Min. Plunge Size	0.00000 *f*
Max. Ramp Radius	0.18000 *f*
DZ/Feed Start	0.10000 *f*

Expand **Machine Parameters** and change **Plunge Feed** and **Side Feed** from 30% to **100**%. In my experience, 100% during ramping works well. Remember that ramping increases cycle times. So you don't want to enter too slow.

☐ **Machine Parameters**	
♀Feed and Spin Calculator	Access
♀Vc (feet/min)	490.87385
♀Spin	5000
♀Feed (inch/min)	50.00000
♀Air Motions	Rapid
♀Plunge Feed (%)	100
♀Side Feed (%)	100
♀Enable Cutter Compensation	No
♀Coolant	Flood
♀Spindle Direction	Clockwise
♀Rotary Axis Preferred Positio	None

Save & Calculate.

Observe the modified entry. It changed to a **helical entry at 3 degrees**. Like a corkscrew, it spirals downward over and over at a 3 degree ramp angle until it reaches the programmed depth of cut. Then it begins machining the pocket.

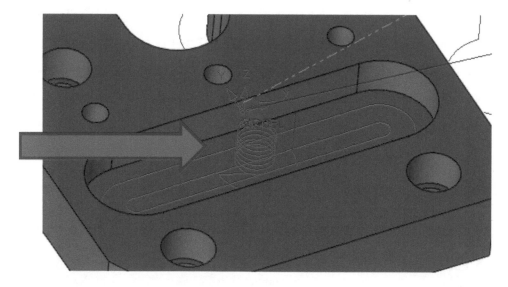

Use the Navigator to observe this new cutterpath.

High Speed Machining:

We're starting to touch on the subject of high speed machining. There are two schools of thought when it comes to machining pockets.

1. The **old school** approach is to program this pocket with many depth passes to reduce wear on the cutter. Plunge angles are left at 90 degrees. Plunge feeds are set to 30%. Each depth pass cuts 0.050 - 0.100 inches deep. And toolpath motion uses a 50% side step.

2. The **High Speed Machining** approach is to cut the pocket in one depth pass (e.g. 0.375 deep). Instead of plunging at 90 degrees at 30%, it ramps in at 3 degrees at 100% feed. The side step, however, must be reduced from 50% to 20% of the tool diameter.

It's hard to believe until you see it in action, but the High Speed Machining approach is much faster and will preserve tool life because it's cutting with the side of the tool instead of burning out the tip. The old school approach wears out the tip of the tool and has a much longer cycle time.

OK, this lesson taught you how to edit procedures and a little about High Speed Machining.

Select **File** and **Save**.

Drilling:

Create a new procedure. Change from 2.5 Axes to **Drill** in the **Main selection**. menu.

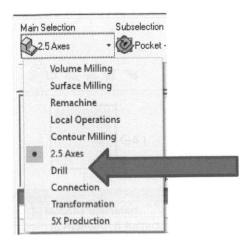

Do not select anything from the Subselection menu.

Like we did before, let's create a new tool first. Select **3/8" End Mill** from **Cutters & Holders** and set the following parameters:

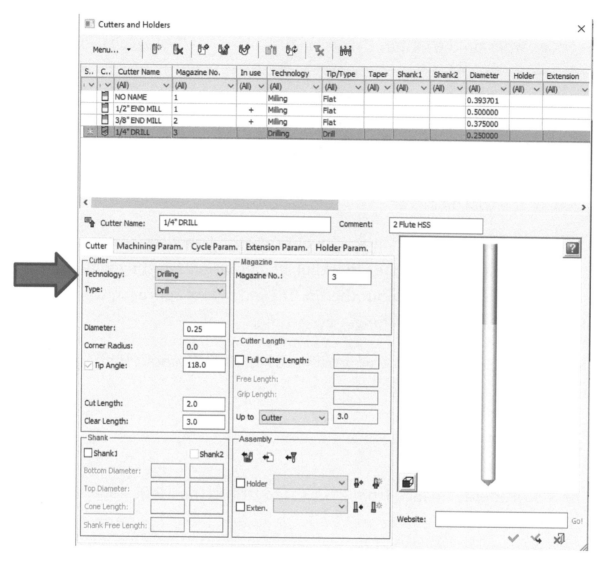

- Cutter Name: **¼" Drill**
- Comment: **2 FLUTE HSS**
- Technology: **Drilling**
- Diameter: **0.25**
- Magazine: **3** (automatically incremented by 1)
- Cut Length: **2** inches
- Clear Length: **3** inches

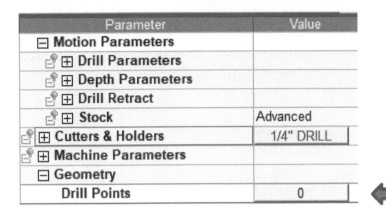

Click the 0 from the Geometry field.

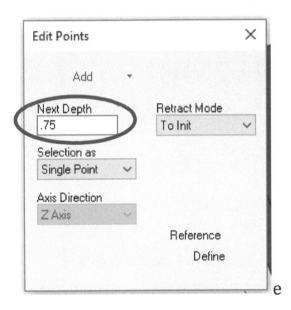

Change **Next Depth** to **0.750**. ***NOTE***: Do not press Enter or the dialog box will disappear. Just typw 0.75 and press the tab key.

Pick Drilling Points and then <exit>.

Notice the prompt in the lower left-hand corner. It's prompting you to pick the points to drill. Hover your cursor over each of the three ¼" diameter circles—one by one—and pick the center of the circle (at the top of the part).

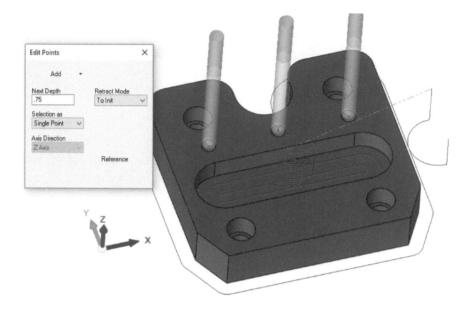

Press the **middle mouse button** to exit point selection.

Expand **Drill Parameters**. Observe that **Spot Drill** is selected. Cimatron offers many drill canned cycles to choose from Spot Drill produces a G81 canned cycle. This cycle drills from the clearance plane to the final depth at a programmed feed. It's the most common drill cycle. When depths are deeper, some programmers prefer to peck drill.

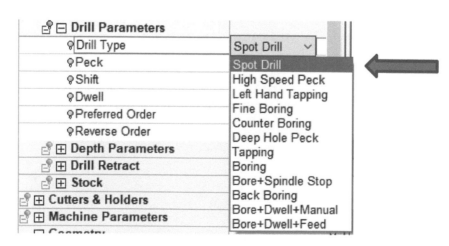

With nothing to change in this heading, minimize the Drill Parameters and expand **Depth Parameters**.

Depth Parameters	
Max. Depth	Calculate
Global Depth Type	Global Depth
Global Depth	0.75000
Depth	Cutter Tip

Click on **Cutter Tip** and observe the options. Because our part is 0.750 thick, we want Cimatron to drill 0.750 deep *plus* the tip of the tool. By selecting **Full Diameter**, Cimatron multiplies the factor 0.3 times the tool diameter, then it adds it to 0.750, for a total depth of 0.750 + 0.075, or 0.825.

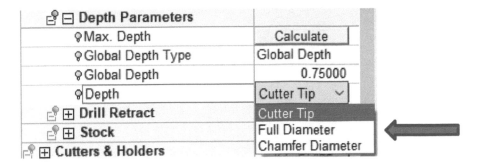

Depth Parameters	
Max. Depth	Calculate
Global Depth Type	Global Depth
Global Depth	0.75000
Depth	Cutter Tip
Drill Retract	Cutter Tip
Stock	Full Diameter
Cutters & Holders	Chamfer Diameter

Be sure to select Full Diameter, then minimize this heading.

Expand **Drill Retract**. Change To Init to **To Retract**. Init refers to the Initial Z plane prior to drilling. To Retract informs the drill to retract to the Clearance Plane—or R-Plane after drilling each hole. R-Plane is short for Retract Plane.

Change the **Delta Retract** to **0.100.** The Delta Init of 0.850 will be ignored.

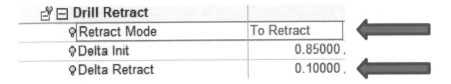

Drill Retract	
Retract Mode	To Retract
Delta Init	0.85000
Delta Retract	0.10000

NOTE: Drilling canned cycles is a large subject to cover and falls outside the scope of this text. Canned cycles are covered in much greater detail in our ATAP 2310 CNC Mill Programming course.

Minimize Drill Retract.

Select **Save & Calculate**.

Select the **Navigator** and observe the toolpath. It drills all three holes, and the tip of the drill breaks through the bottom. However, for through holes it's customary to break through an additional 0.100 to allow the steel chip to bend over and break. If the tool doesn't not break through enough, the bottom of the hole work hardens and becomes difficult to hand deburr.

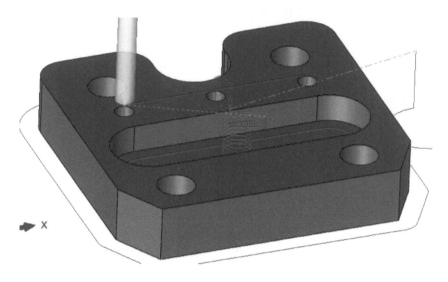

Rotate to a front view, single step the toolpath to the bottom of any of the holes to see that the tool doesn't not contain the additional 0.100:

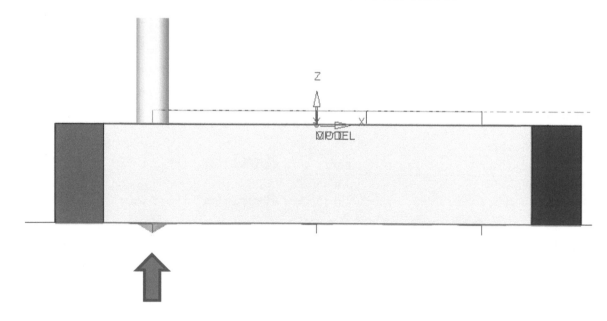

Exit the Navigator.

Edit the Drill procedure (double-click it or right-click Edit).

Expand **Depth Parameters** and change 0.750 to **0.850**

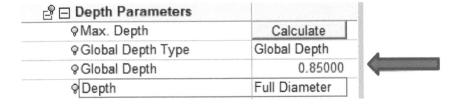

Save & Calculate

Select **Navigator** and observe:

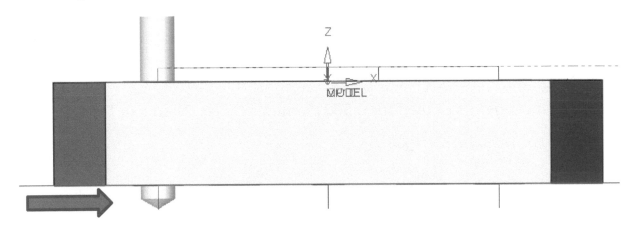

Exit the Navigator.

Drill four 0.375 diameter through holes:

Create a second drill **Procedure**.

Click **3** in the Geometry field.

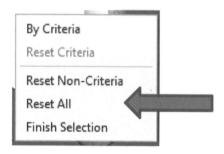

Right-click in the graphics area and select **Reset All**.

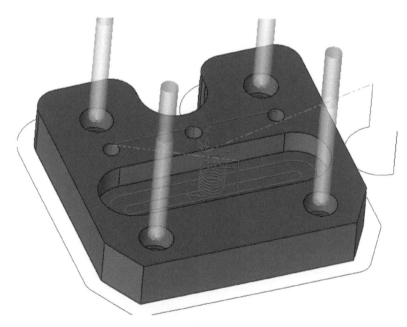

Pick the center points of the four 0.500 diameter circles. Then exit (middle mouse button).

Create a **new tool** with t following paramaters:

- 3/8" Drill
- Magazine #4
- Diameter = 0.375

Save & Calculate.

Select Navigator and observe that it looks well.

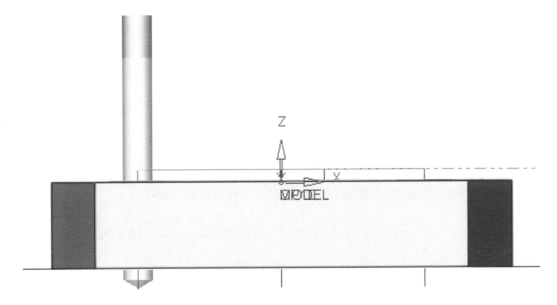

The final step is to **counterbore** the four holes with a ½" end mill 0.387 deep.

Exit the Navigator.

Create a new **Drill Procedure**.

Select the 3/8" DRILL field and choose the ½" **END MILL** (TOOL 1) from the tools list. This is the same cutter we used to profile the outside shape in step 1.

In the **Depth Parameters** panel, change Full Diameter to **Cutter Tip**, and change the **Global Depth to 0.387**:

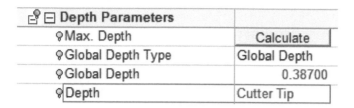

Depth Parameters	
Max. Depth	Calculate
Global Depth Type	Global Depth
Global Depth	0.38700
Depth	Cutter Tip

Select Machine Parameters and change the feed rate to **10**

Save & Calculate

Save your file.

Select the **Machining Simulation** icon from the NC Wizard.

Click the double arrow in the middle to transfer all Available Procedures to the Simulation Sequence.

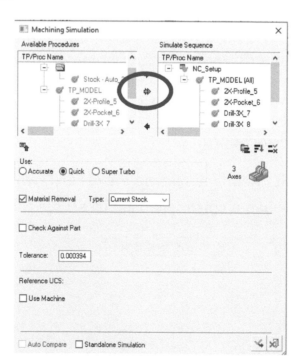

Press **OK** to launch the Simulation package.

Press the **Movie Camera** icon to simulate.

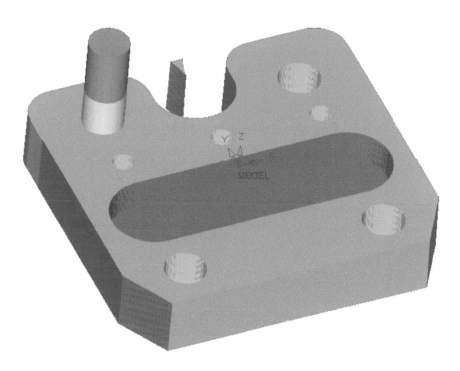

Upon completion, select the **Exit Simulator** icon from the wizard on the far left side at the bottom of the screen.

Congratulations. This completes this CAM exercise. It took you a little further than CAM exercise 1 by introducing you to toolpath editing, drilling, and simulation.

Chapter 9: Drafting

Drafting Exercise 1: Cardholder Base

Cimtaron has a powerful drafting package. It can be used to create anything from shop floor drawings to full blown assembly drawings. And like the NC package, Drafting is fully associative to the model. So, if and when the model changes, the drawings can be updated to include the design changes.

To keep things simple at this introductory level, we'll bypass drawing templates and go right to creating views and dimensions.

Launch a new session of Cimatron.

Select **File > Drawing_inch**:

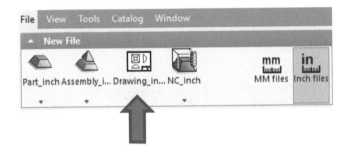

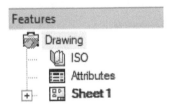

This displays a blank page on the right, and some menus on the left in the Feature Tree. Notice the default coordinate system is **ISO** (International Standards Organization). If you remember from your drafting classes, this represents 1st angle projection—the European style of dimensioning.

Double-click on ISO and change it to **ANSI** (American National Standards Institute). This represents 3rd angle projection—which is what most of us want to use in America. Then press **OK**.

You're ready to create your first view to dimension. Right-click in the graphics area on the right. Select View Creation. It then displays the View Creation dialog.

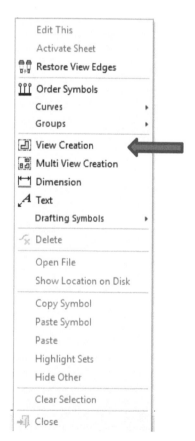

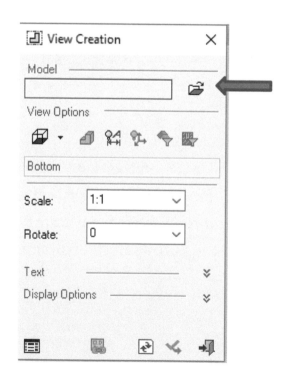

Click on the **Open a Cimatron File** icon from the View Creation dialog and select **Cardholder Base** from the file navigator. *NOTE*: If you don't see your hard drive, flash drive, or your file in the navigator, press the **F5** function key to refresh the Cimatron File Navigator. This happens quite often.

After opening the file, digitize anywhere in the graphics screen to load the first view.

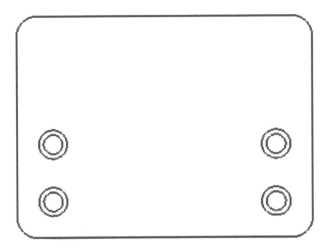

Simple1

This file has come in upside down from what we want to see, so select **downward arrow** from the **Simple View Projection Type**.

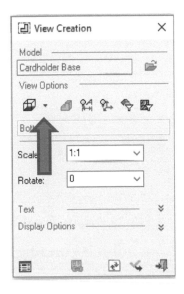
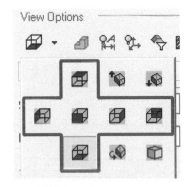

Your view options are encompassed in red. Select the TOP view and observe the new—correct orientation.

Expand the Text options and change the Position type to None. This will eliminate the silly text box under the top view.

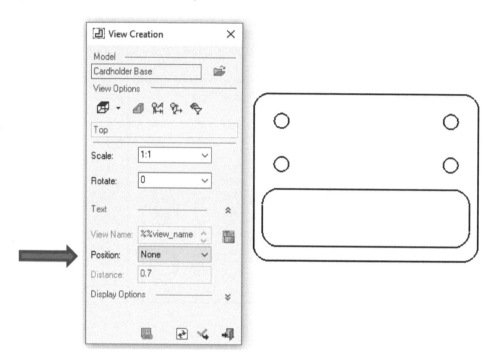

Finally, press the **Apply** button (green checkmark), followed by the **Close** icon in the lower right-hand corner of the dialog.

Dimension:

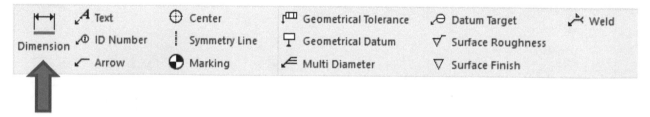

Pick near the bottom of the two vertical lines that define the inside pocket. Then digitize below the part to create the dimension. Notice the default condition is to dimension 2 places behind the decimal point. However, we want three.

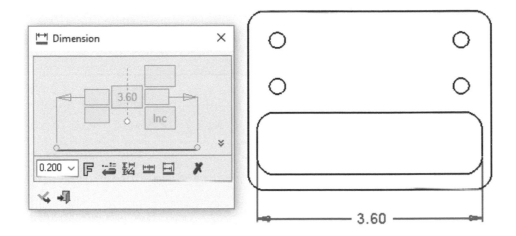

Pick the middle box (labeled 3.6) in the Dimension dialog.

Change Dim. ## to **Dim, ###**.

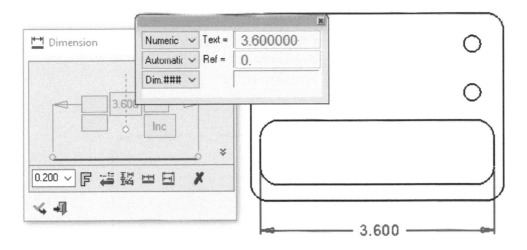

Since the text height of 0.200 appears to be OK, press the green checkmark.

Next, dimension the width of the box by picking near the bottom ends of the two outside vertical lines. Then press **OK** (green checkmark).

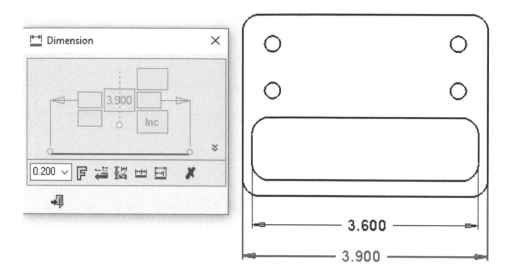

Add the **2.950 dimension** near the top and press **OK**. Note: Be careful to select the centers of the two circles.

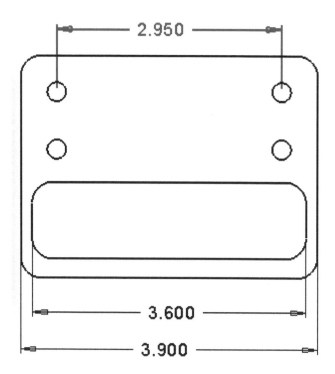

Add the **0.150 dimension** in the lower right-and corner. Notice it includes a note, though. It reads **0.150 (TYP.)**. To accomplish this, click in the middle text box in the right-most column and type (TYP.) Click on the dimension to adjust it cosmetically. Then press OK.

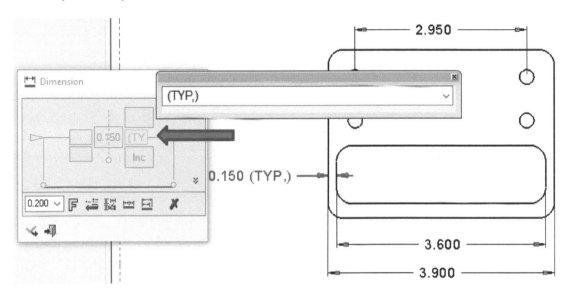

Add the **0.475 (TYP.)** dimension.

Add the vertical dimensions as shown on the right.

NOTE: When you add the 0.200 dimension, click on the middle field in the right-hand column and remove the (TYP.) string.

You might also want to change the text height from 0.200 to 0.175 to make it fit in better.

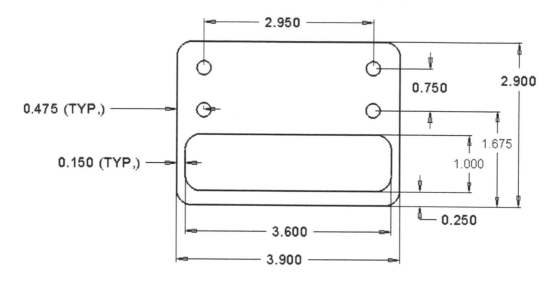

Notice the counterbores from the backside are not visible as hidden lines in this view. This is because Cimatron defaults to not showing them.

Double-click **Attributes** from the Feature Tree. Then checkmark **Model Hidden,** change the color to **black** (from grayscale)**,** and press **OK**.

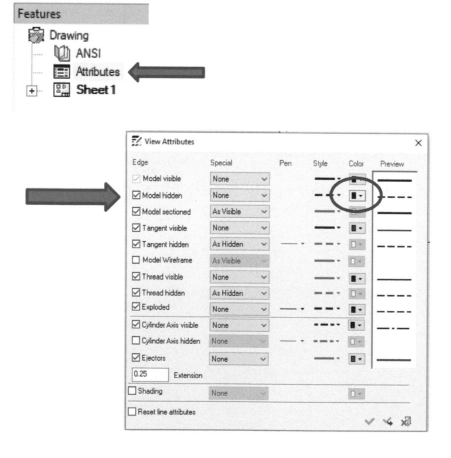

Dimension the ¼" hole as follows. (Pick the ¼" hole—not the 3/8")

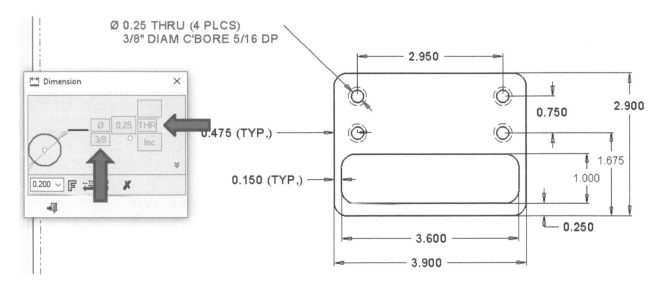

NOTE: The first line of the dimension automatically includes the 0.250 diameter. So type in **THRU (4 PLCS)** to the right of it. Then type **3/8" DIAM C'BORE 5/16 DP** in the bottom row of the left-hand column.

Dimension the **0.275** corner radii as follows.

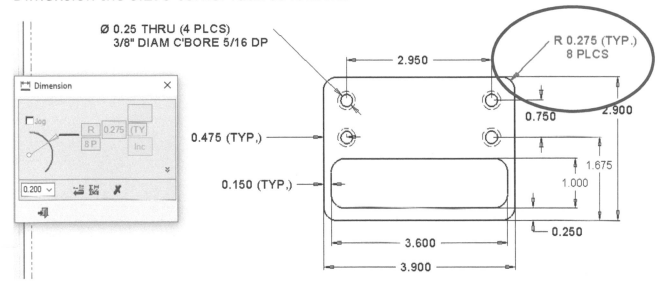

Now let's **add the right view**.

Close the Dimension dialog.

Right-click in a blank space of the graphics area and select **View Creation**.

Pick anywhere on the existing view (anywhere along an edge). Then digitize to the right of the top view. Cimatron aligns the right view to the right with the proper orientation and hidden lines.

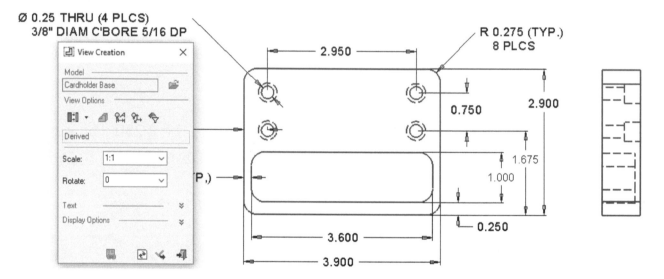

Select **OK** and **Close** the View Creation dialog.

Add three dimensions to this view as shown.

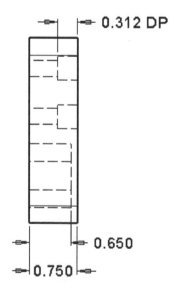

This completes this exercise.

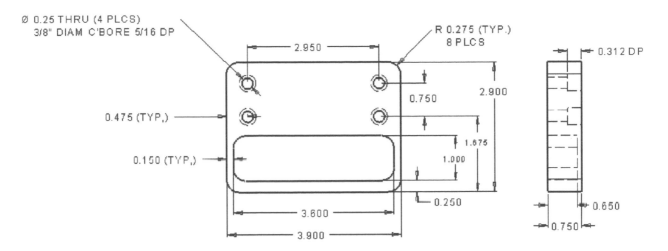

Select **File > Save as Main**. Name your drawing **Cardholder_Base_DWG**.